The Glassblower's Gamble

Timeless Parables on Craft, Risk, and What a Fortune Is Actually Made Of

Eleanor Voss

First edition, 2026

Published by Eleanor Voss

Contents

I. The Weight of the Long Kiln

I was nineteen the first winter I kept the Long Kiln alone, and that first night taught me everything I needed to know about the precarious balance between heat, time, and control. The fire wasn't just fuel; it was a constant reminder of what could be gained—and lost—in a single moment.

Glass does not become glass in the furnace. It becomes glass in the cooling. A piece pulled molten from the furnace and shaped by breath and iron is, in that moment, still full of a strain no eye can see — the outside skin already stiffening in the cooler air while the deep glass beneath it is still soft, still moving, still fighting to catch up. If you let that piece cool on its own, in open air, the outer skin hardens fast and the inner glass keeps shrinking behind it, and the two mismatched speeds pull against each other until, sometimes in an hour, sometimes in three weeks, the whole piece simply comes apart along a line no one could have predicted, for a reason no one standing there at the time would ever see.

The Long Kiln exists to prevent exactly this. It is a low, wide oven built of the same stone as the workshops around it, banked with coals that burn low and steady rather than hot, and its whole purpose is to bring a piece down from the furnace's full heat to the cold of the outside world slowly enough that the inside and the outside of the glass cool at nearly the same rate, with no mismatched strain left locked inside it. A piece properly annealed in the Long Kiln can be dropped, within reason, and merely chip. A piece pulled too soon can shatter from a draft.

My father kept the Long Kiln before me, and his mother before him, and the post has always come with one piece of advice passed down essentially unchanged: you cannot see which pieces will fail.

You can only see which pieces were given enough time.

The Long Kiln itself is older than any single family that has ever tended it, built jointly, generations ago, by the earliest glassblowers to settle that stretch of the cove, on the simple and practical recognition that not every workshop could afford its own private annealing furnace, and that a piece cooled too quickly in the open air was a piece wasted regardless of who had blown it. It is governed, even now, by a handful of rules so old that no one living remembers who first set them down, though every keeper learns them the same way: no piece leaves before its full time regardless of who asks or what they offer; the fire is banked the same way every night, checked at the same three intervals, by whoever holds the post, without exception for weather, feast days, or grief; and any keeper who breaks the first rule forfeits the post entirely, a punishment so rarely invoked in the kiln's long history that I know of only one keeper, generations before my father's time, who ever actually triggered it, and whose name has been quietly left out of the post's own oral history ever since, as though the trade itself preferred simply to forget him rather than remember what he'd done.

I did not fully appreciate, my first winter alone at the fire, how much responsibility those rules actually placed on a single pair of hands. A private furnace answers only to its own owner, who can weigh the risk of pulling a piece early against his own tolerance for loss and decide accordingly. The Long Kiln answers to every glassblower in the quarter who trusts it with their work, most of whom cannot see inside it at any given hour and have no way of checking, themselves, whether their piece is truly ready or has simply been declared ready by a keeper eager to clear space for the next batch. That trust, I came to understand fairly early, was the entire product the Long Kiln actually sold, in the same way that a public scale in a very different city, in an earlier book of mine, sold nothing but the confidence that its reading could be trusted without checking — and it required, I learned within that first winter, almost nothing at all to lose.

Corliss was, at that point in his life, still building the reputation that would eventually let him afford the very showroom his later troubles would be built around, and a commission from a merchant's household as prominent as the one asking for these goblets represented, for a young glassblower still establishing himself, precisely the kind of custom that could carry a whole workshop's fortunes forward for years if handled well, or set them back considerably if handled poorly. I understood, even at nineteen, why the temptation to bend the rule for this particular commission ran deeper in him than an ordinary rush job would have. That understanding did not change my answer. It only made giving it harder.

The winter I mean to tell you about, this same Corliss Fen — young then, ambitious, not yet the man his later troubles would make of him, a story I will tell elsewhere in this book — brought me a set of eight goblets, commissioned by that merchant's household for a wedding feast three days off, and asked whether they could be pulled from the kiln early. They had been in less than a full day, well short of the two full days a piece of that thickness needed, but the feast could not be moved, and Corliss stood in my doorway with the particular pleading calm of a man who already knows the answer he is going to be given and has decided to ask anyway.

I told him no. He asked why one day should matter so much, when the goblets already looked, to any eye in the workshop, entirely finished — clear, sound, no visible flaw anywhere on them. I told him what my father had told me, which is that a piece of glass does not look unfinished when its cooling has been rushed. It looks exactly like a finished piece, right up until it isn't one anymore, and there is no way to tell the difference by looking, only by waiting the time the glass actually needs regardless of what the surface shows you.

He did not simply accept this the first time I said it. Few people do, and I have never held that against any of them, because a rule that asks a person to trust an invisible process over the plain evidence of their own eyes is a genuinely hard rule to obey the first time it costs them something. Corliss lifted one of the goblets from the rack himself, turned it in the lamplight, held it up so I could see clean through it to the stone wall behind. "Look at it," he said. "Tell me honestly what you see wrong with it." I told him I saw nothing wrong with it, and that this was exactly the trouble — that nothing wrong with it was precisely what a piece looked like an hour before it failed as well as ten years before it didn't, and that the only thing that told the two apart was time already spent, not time yet to come. He set the goblet down harder than he needed to, not from anger exactly, more from the particular frustration of a young man who has just been told that his own careful eyes are not equal to the question in front of him.

I offered him what comfort I could, which was not much. I told him that my father had lost, by his own account, nearly a third of one particularly hard winter's income turning away rushed pieces exactly this way, and had not once, in the whole of his career, regretted a single refusal, though he had regretted, twice, relenting. "Twice," Corliss repeated, as though the number itself might be an argument in his favor. I told him it was, if anything, an argument the other way — that even a careful man who mostly held the line had proof, twice over, of what happened the times he didn't.

Corliss did not take the goblets. To his credit — and I want to say this plainly, because the rest of his story in this book will not always show him at his best — he went back to the merchant's household and told them honestly that the goblets would not be ready in time for the feast, and offered instead a simpler set he could finish and anneal properly within the three days he had. The merchant was annoyed. Corliss lost, that week, some part of the fee he had hoped for. The eight goblets finished their two full days in the Long Kiln and were delivered a week late, to a household that had already half-decided to think less of him for the delay.

I remember the particular walk he took back to my doorway the evening after that conversation with the merchant, because he did not have to make it — the decision was already settled, the simpler set already promised in the goblets' place — and yet he came anyway, and stood in the same spot he'd stood in that morning, and said nothing at all for a while, watching the coals through the small iron door. Finally he said, "I keep thinking I should feel better about this than I do." I told him that the feeling would not arrive on any schedule he could plan for, and that in my experience it rarely arrived before the outcome did — that a right choice, made honestly, before anyone could prove it was right, mostly just felt like a loss for a good long while, and that this was, in fact, precisely why so few people managed to make it. Anyone can hold the line once the proof has already arrived. The whole difficulty of the thing is holding it before the proof exists at all, on nothing but a rule someone older passed down and a fire that has never once explained itself.

The merchant's household, for its part, did not let the matter rest quietly. Word went round Ledger Row — I mean the harbor road, though the habit of certain phrases follows a storyteller from one book to the next, I find, whether she means it to or not — that Corliss Fen had turned down a paying commission over what several of the merchant's own kitchen staff described, not unkindly, as "a day the goblets probably didn't even need." A rival glassblower two streets over, a competent but unremarkable craftsman named Ossett Bray, took the household's overflow custom for the season that followed, and made a point, more than once, of mentioning to anyone who'd listen that he, at least, understood how to meet a deadline.

I tell you this story first, before any of the others, because of what happened eleven years later, at a different feast, held by that same merchant's grown daughter, using those same eight goblets, still whole, still clear, having survived a decade of ordinary household use without a single crack — while the simpler set Corliss had rushed through in three days for the original feast had all shattered, one by one, within the first two years, exactly the way glass shatters when it has been asked to cool faster than it wanted to. The merchant's household, by the time of the daughter's own feast, had come to understand something about Corliss's work that they had not understood at the time of his first delay: that the goblets which arrived late were the ones still standing, and the ones that arrived on time were the ones now gone.

Ossett Bray's own rushed set, as it happened, had a harder second act than Corliss's slower one. The simpler goblets he supplied that season for the wedding feast held well enough through the first year, long enough that the story of Corliss's refusal had mostly faded from casual conversation along the harbor road, and Ossett built, on the strength of that single well-timed commission and a handful that followed it, a modest reputation of his own as a glassblower who could be relied upon in a pinch. It was not until the household's own daughter, grown by then, went looking for a matching ninth goblet to replace one lost to an ordinary household accident, that anyone thought to compare the two sets side by side again — Corliss's eight, still whole, still catching the light the same clean way they always had, and Ossett's remaining pieces, thinned by then to five out of the original set, the other three having failed quietly, one by one, over years nobody had bothered connecting back to a single rushed winter.

I do not think Corliss knew, standing in my doorway that winter morning, that the choice he was making would matter eleven years later to anyone. I do not think most people, standing at the edge of a choice like that one, ever do. He simply understood, that morning, a single fact about the fire he worked with: that it did not care how badly he needed the goblets finished by Thursday, and that no amount of wanting a thing sooner would make it actually be sooner without a cost attached, hidden somewhere inside the glass, waiting for a moment no one could predict.

Ossett Bray himself, to his credit, did not vanish from the trade once the comparison finally caught up with him. He came to me once, some years after the merchant's daughter's feast had made the two sets' fates common knowledge along the harbor road, and asked, with a humility I had not expected from him, whether I thought a glassblower could unlearn a habit of rushing once it had already cost him a reputation. I told him I did not know, having never watched anyone attempt it from quite so public a starting point, but that the Long Kiln's own rules had not once asked whether a man deserved a second chance before agreeing to anneal his work properly if he brought it to the fire honestly and waited out the full time. He took the answer, I think, as more encouragement than I intended it to be, and to his lasting credit he did, in fact, spend the following decade rebuilding a slower, more careful practice, bringing every piece to the Long Kiln rather than risking his own private methods again, until by the end of his working life the harbor road spoke of him, if not as warmly as it spoke of Corliss, at least no longer as the man whose goblets hadn't held.

A fortune rushed does not look rushed. It looks, for a while, exactly like a fortune that was built properly — clear, sound, admired by everyone who sees only the surface of it. The strain is invisible until the day it isn't, and by then the person holding the pieces rarely remembers, or ever knew, which choice years earlier put it there.

If you let that piece cool on its own, in open air…

The kiln doesn't just *make* glass; it reveals the inherent fragility within, a lesson Wren Calder would soon learn in the relentless grind of sifting sand.

II. The Sandsifter's Discipline

Have you ever considered how much of an object's value isn't in the material itself, but in the hours, skill, and story woven into its creation? In the Cinderquay, that question wasn't academic; it was survival.

Wren Calder's first morning at it, she was eleven years old and angry about nearly everything. Her hands were still soft from a childhood spent nowhere near a furnace. The basket they gave her was woven so tight the sand leaked through anyway if you looked at it wrong. The beach stretched out in both directions, endless and gray, and somewhere out there—she had no idea where, exactly—was the particular grade of sand that would satisfy Beck Thorne, the glassblower who'd taken her on because his workshop needed an extra pair of hands, not because he'd seen anything special in her.

She filled her first basket by midmorning, hauled it back to the workshop, and watched Beck dump it straight onto the discard heap without a word. Too coarse. She went back out.

The second basket took until early afternoon. Beck held a handful up to the light, squinted, and dumped it. Shell fragments, he said. You're not looking.

The third basket she brought him just before sunset, her shoulders aching in places she hadn't known could ache. This one he kept. He didn't say it was good. He said, "That'll do for tomorrow's batch," and went back to the furnace, and Wren understood, standing there in the doorway with sand still under her fingernails, that she had just signed herself up for roughly a thousand more mornings exactly like this one before anyone would let her near the actual work.

Most apprentices treat those years as a sentence to be served. Wren treated them—though she could never quite explain why, even decades later when I asked—as an actual craft.

She began sorting her sand not just for coarseness, which was all Beck asked of her, but for the particular quality of white it produced once melted. She noticed, long before anyone told her to notice, that sand taken from different stretches of the cove, at different depths, after different weather, yielded glass with subtly different clarities. A careful sifter, patient enough to sort for this as well as for simple impurity, could hand a glassblower sand that started the whole process half a step ahead of anyone else's.

She kept a private record of it.

Nobody asked her to. She scratched notes onto a slate she wiped and rewrote each season—which stretch of shore, which depth, which weather produced the clearest results—until by her sixth year she could walk the cove after any given storm and tell, just by looking, roughly which patch would sift clean and which wouldn't. No one else in the Cinderquay possessed this skill, because no one else had spent six years caring about a question nobody had asked her to answer.

You might be wondering what the point of all that was. Wren wondered the same thing, I suspect, more than once during those years. Sand is sand. You sift it, someone melts it, it becomes glass. Why track which storm, which tide, which angle of shore? Why keep a slate full of notes on something as simple as picking up handfuls of ground quartz and running them through a screen?

Here's why it mattered.

There was an afternoon in Wren's fifth year—she described it to me decades later as the moment she first understood what her private accounting was actually worth—when a merchant's household commissioned a set of clear serving bowls from Beck Thorne's workshop for an important occasion. They specified, in a way most customers never bothered to, that the glass be as flawlessly clear as any bowl they had ever purchased from any workshop in the quarter.

Beck, uncertain which of his usual sand suppliers could meet the standard on short notice, asked Wren—almost as an afterthought—whether she had any thoughts on the matter.

She walked that same evening directly to a stretch of shore she had marked on her slate two winters before as producing an unusually pure yield after a particular kind of autumn storm. She dug there specifically, rather than at the workshop's ordinary gathering spot. She returned with sand that produced, when melted, a clarity that made even Beck pause and hold the trial piece up to the light longer than he needed to.

He asked her how she had known to look there.

She told him the truth. That she had been keeping track, quietly, for years.

Something shifted in the way he looked at her after that. As though noticing, for the first time, that the girl who fetched his sand might actually know something about it that he didn't.

But here's what I want you to feel before we go any further, because the rest of this chapter won't land right if you don't: the cost of skipping this part. Not the theoretical cost. The actual one, the kind that shows up years later in ways you can't patch over with hard work or talent or good intentions.

Perrin Sable apprenticed alongside Wren those same years. Same beach, same baskets, same resentful mornings hauling sand he had no interest in understanding. He was faster than Wren at nearly everything—quicker hands, surer instincts, the kind of natural facility that makes masters take early notice. A master did take notice, pulled him from the sand in his fourth year rather than his seventh, and for a long while afterward this looked, to everyone in the quarter, like the better outcome.

Perrin got three extra years at the blowpipe. Three years of actual glassblowing while Wren was still on the beach with her slate and her private accounting that nobody had asked for.

By his ninth year at the pipe, Perrin was producing work that anyone in the Cinderquay would have called accomplished. Technically skilled. Consistent. Saleable. Beautiful, even, in the way a well-executed piece of craft is always beautiful.

And stuck.

He couldn't figure out why. His hands were as good as they'd ever been—better, if anything, after nine years of daily practice. He understood annealing, understood timing, understood the particular rhythm of breath and heat that turns molten glass into something deliberate rather than accidental. He was doing everything right.

But his pieces plateaued in a way that puzzled him for years. Good, but never quite reaching the particular clear brilliance that buyers began—without being able to explain why—to associate specifically with Wren's work rather than his own.

It wasn't a dramatic difference. That's what made it so hard to pin down. If you held one of Perrin's bowls next to one of Wren's, both were lovely. Both were well-made. But Wren's had something—a quality of light, a depth of clarity—that Perrin's didn't, and the more he tried to close that gap through sheer effort at the pipe, the more he realized the gap wasn't at the pipe at all.

It was in the sand. It had always been in the sand.

What do you lose when you skip the boring part?

You lose the part that compounds.

I've watched this same pattern play out in a dozen other trades, in a dozen other workshops, and the shape of it is always the same. Someone gets an early start, and it looks like a gift. Someone else spends years on the unglamorous foundation work that nobody celebrates, and it looks like a waste. And then ten years pass, and the person with the early start hits a ceiling they can't explain, and the person who stayed with the boring part for longer than anyone thought reasonable is still quietly compounding gains from knowledge nobody else bothered to build.

Perrin told me once, years later—after he'd finally understood what he was missing and gone back to learn it—that the hardest part wasn't admitting Wren knew something he didn't. The hardest part was realizing he'd traded away the one thing he couldn't buy back: the years.

"I used to think patience was something Wren had and I didn't," he said, "the way some people are simply born more patient than others. It took me a long time to understand that what she had wasn't a virtue exactly. It was three extra years of a specific, unglamorous kind of attention that I had traded away for an early start, and that no quantity of patience applied afterward could fully buy back, because the sand doesn't care how patient you're willing to be about it now. It only cares how long you actually spent with it when you were eleven."

There was a game the apprentices used to play at the tideline, in the idle stretches between one sifting task and the next—a competition to see who could fill a small woven basket with clean sand the fastest, judged not by any adult but simply by whichever apprentices happened to be working the shore that morning.

Perrin nearly always won it. His hands were quicker and surer than any of the others', and he took a boyish pride in the winning that Wren remembered clearly even decades later.

She never once won the race herself.

She told me she stopped trying fairly early, once she noticed that the fastest fillers were rarely sorting for anything beyond coarseness, and that slowing down enough to notice the finer differences cost her every single race but taught her, over those same years, something the races themselves were never measuring at all.

"Perrin thought I'd simply given up competing," she said. "I had. I just hadn't given up learning, and it took me a long time to understand those weren't the same thing."

What are you racing toward that isn't actually the thing that matters?

I'm not asking because I think you'll answer it right now. I'm asking because I want you to sit with the question for a minute, the way Wren sat with the sand, before we move on to what she did with all those years nobody thought were going anywhere.

When Wren finally took up a blowpipe herself, in her seventh year, she was no faster or more naturally gifted with her hands than a dozen other apprentices her age who had spent those same years actually blowing glass rather than sifting it. But her glass, from her very first pieces, came out of the furnace with a clarity that older glassblowers in the quarter noticed and could not immediately explain.

They assumed, reasonably enough, that clarity was a matter of skill at the pipe. They had no idea that half of it had already been decided on the beach, years before, by a girl with a slate.

Old Rasmus Ilde saw it before most people did. Rasmus was a retired ship's glazier who spent his last years drinking spiced water in the Cinderquay's square and offering opinions nobody had asked for, and he told me once, watching Perrin and Wren work through adjoining doorways on an ordinary afternoon, "Perrin blows glass better than Wren did at his age. But Wren understands the sand better than Perrin understands anything, and sooner or later, in this trade, that is the difference that shows."

Rasmus had spent his own working decades aboard trading vessels, glazing cabin windows and lantern housings in conditions considerably rougher than any furnace room in the Cinderquay. Shipboard glazing had taught him the same lesson from a different direction, the hard way, twice.

"The first ship I served on," he said, "I learned to patch a cracked pane fast, because a captain does not care how a repair was made, only that it holds through the next storm. I got very good, very quick, at fast patches."

He paused there, the way people do when they're about to tell you the part of the story that cost them something.

"It took me four more years on a second ship, under a glazier who refused to let me touch a pane until I understood the wood grain it sat in, the give of the frame around it, the salt air's particular way of working a seal loose over a season rather than a night—it took those four years before I understood that the fast patches I'd been so proud of were the reason that first ship's windows needed constant re-patching, season after season, while the second ship's, glazed slower and with more understanding underneath the hands doing it, held for a decade without complaint."

He said he saw the same two glaziers in Perrin and Wren every time he watched them work, though neither of them was doing anything wrong exactly. Only building two different kinds of foundation, one of which would show its limits later than the other.

I remember the particular morning I first understood what Wren was actually doing out there, because I happened to be walking the shore myself, checking the Long Kiln's woodpile after a delivery, and found her crouched at the tideline before first light, running a handful of wet sand between her fingers the way another child her age might have played with it—except that she was murmuring something under her breath as she did it. A kind of private accounting. Numbers and directions. North spit or south hollow. Before-storm or after.

I didn't understand it at the time. It only made sense years later, once I had seen the slate itself and the small careful marks covering it.

She startled when she noticed me watching, the way any child caught at an odd private habit might, and I asked her, more out of idle curiosity than any real interest, what she was doing.

"Learning where the good sand hides," she said, as though this were the most ordinary answer in the world, and went back to her sifting without waiting to see whether I believed her.

Beck Thorne, her own master at the time, was a competent but unremarkable glassblower who had taken her on mostly because his workshop needed an extra pair of hands rather than out of any particular eye for talent. He never once asked to see the slate, and would not, I think, have understood its value if he had. He measured Wren's usefulness those first years by how quickly and how much sand she delivered to his furnace room each morning, and by that measure alone she was simply an adequate apprentice, neither faster nor slower than the two boys who had come up alongside her.

It did not occur to Beck to wonder why his own glass, in those years, came out very slightly clearer than it had before Wren joined him. The improvement was too gradual and too small, season to season, for a busy man to notice happening at all.

Perrin did eventually go back to it—not sifting sand himself, which by then would have cost him years he no longer had to spend, but seeking out Wren directly, in his ninth year at the pipe, and asking her, with the particular humility of a talented man who has finally located the one thing he is missing, whether she would teach him what she knew about the cove.

She did, over several patient seasons, and his work improved for it. Considerably.

But he told me once, years later, that he never fully closed the gap between what she understood about the sand from six years of daily attention and what he had absorbed from a handful of seasons of catching up.

"I got the shortcut version," he said. "It was better than nothing. It was not the same as having actually walked the beach myself, every morning, for six years, before I ever wanted to."

A skill that compounds looks, for years, exactly like time wasted. A slate full of notes nobody asked for. A task everyone else is eager to leave behind.

A skill that plateaus looks, for those same years, exactly like talent rewarded early.

The difference rarely shows itself in the first decade. It shows itself in the second, when one kind of foundation is still quietly paying interest and the other has nothing left to draw on but the hands that built it.

Wren herself, in her own final working years, kept the same habit that had started her whole career—walking the shore before first light more mornings than not, long after she had any practical need to sift sand herself rather than delegate the task to an apprentice, the way Beck Thorne once delegated it to her.

I asked her once why she still went, given how little the workshop actually required it of her by then.

"I am not really checking the sand anymore," she admitted. "I think I am checking whether I still remember how to notice something nobody has asked me to notice. It is a harder habit to lose than you'd think, once it's properly set in you, and I have found I would rather keep exercising it on sand than let it go slack from disuse."

She was quiet for a moment, running a handful of the morning's sand between her fingers the way she had done at eleven, at seventeen, at thirty-five, the same private motion she had probably made ten thousand times by then.

"Besides," she said, "you never know when the cove is going to teach you something new."

What happens when the thing everyone else rushed past turns out to be the thing that keeps teaching you, decade after decade, long after you thought you'd learned everything it had to offer?

The answer, at least in her case, was that it became something closer to a language than a hobby. She could read the beach now the way a forester reads bark, the way a sailor reads the colour of distant water. She knew which storms left which patterns, how the moon's phase showed up three days later in the layering, what it meant when she found a particular type of shell crushed at a particular angle. She had developed, without intending to, an entire vocabulary for something most people glanced at once and never thought about again.

And it was this vocabulary—not the collection itself, not the objects she'd gathered—that turned out to be the real inheritance of all those years.

Because once you have spent that long noticing one thing properly, you begin to notice other things properly too. She found she could no longer walk through a room without seeing how the light moved across it. She could not listen to someone speak without hearing the silences between their sentences. The practice had generalised. What had begun as a child's curiosity about sand had matured into a broader disposition toward the world: a habit of sustained attention, an expectation that the obvious was probably concealing something worth finding.

This, I think, is what most people miss when they dismiss repetitive practice as tedious or unambitious. They see someone doing the same thing year after year and assume stagnation. They do not see that repetition, when pursued with genuine attention, does not flatten experience—it deepens it. The tenth year of looking is not the same as the first. The ten thousandth sift is not a copy of the hundredth. You are not doing the same thing again; you are doing it differently, because you are different, because the practice has changed you in ways that only the practice itself can reveal.

She told me once that the hardest part was not the discipline itself, but the quiet indifference she encountered when she tried to explain it. People assumed she had exhausted the subject years ago. They could not imagine what there was left to learn from something so ordinary, so bounded, so repetitive. And she had stopped trying to convince them. She understood by then that the value of her practice was not something she could summarise in a sentence. It was cumulative, textured, layered in exactly the way the sand was layered—and just as difficult to convey to someone who had not done the sifting themselves.

What she had built was not a collection. It was a capacity. The capacity to stay with something long enough to move past the surface, past the easy insights, past the point where most people declare a thing finished and turn toward something new. She had learned what lives on the other side of boredom, which is not more boredom but a kind of clarity that only comes from refusing to look away.

And so she kept returning to the cove, not because she was stuck, but because she had learned something the rest of us spend our whole lives trying to remember: that depth is not found by covering more ground, but by standing still long enough to notice what you are standing on.

But discipline alone isn't enough to conquer the furnace – Isbet Voll proved that true mastery lies in unlocking secrets others can't even perceive.

III. The Rival's Blue Flame

The sand on the beaches of Ashmere isn't uniform. Each grain holds a unique composition, a subtle variation that can make or break a batch of glass—and the glassblowers of the Cinderquay knew exactly where to find the best.

The blue belonged to Isbet Voll, a master glassblower of considerable and quiet reputation, achieved through a mineral mixture she had developed across some fifteen years of private experiment and not once explained to anyone outside her own workshop — not out of any particular secrecy for its own sake, she always insisted, but because the mixture had been arrived at through so much accumulated trial that she genuinely was not certain she could explain it in words even if she wanted to; her hands knew proportions her tongue had never learned to name.

She had begun the experiment, she told me once, not out of any grand ambition but from a much smaller and more personal irritation: a blue she had seen as a young woman, on a single traveling merchant's cart passing briefly through the Cinderquay, that no local workshop could match, and that vanished with the merchant before she thought to ask him where it came from or how it was made.

She described the cart to me in enough detail, decades later, that I suspect the memory had lost very little of its original vividness across all those intervening years — a modest wooden cart, nothing grand, carrying mostly ordinary trade goods, with a single small blue vase set almost carelessly among the rest, as though its owner had no particular idea what he was carrying. Isbet had been sixteen, running an errand for her own mother, and had stopped in the street simply to look at it, the way a person sometimes stops without quite deciding to. She asked the merchant where the vase had come from. He told her, if she recalled correctly, some distant town whose name she had since forgotten, or perhaps never properly caught in the first place, being too absorbed in the color itself to attend closely to the answer. By the time she thought to ask a second, more useful question, the cart had already moved on, and she never saw the merchant, or anything resembling that particular blue, again in all her life — until she made it herself, fifteen years later, out of nothing but memory and an enormous quantity of ruined batches. She spent the better part of fifteen years, on and off, chasing a memory of a color she had seen exactly once, for perhaps a quarter of an hour, as a girl of sixteen. The blue she eventually produced was not, by her own honest admission, identical to the merchant's — she had no way of knowing whether it was even close, having only her own memory to measure it against — but it became, over those fifteen years, unmistakably and entirely her own, in a way the original never could have been even if she had somehow reproduced it exactly.

The glassblower it nearly ruined was a younger man named Kester Doune, who worked two doors down from Isbet's shop and had, for reasons even he could not fully account for later, become fixated on matching her blue almost from the first season he saw it. He was, by every honest measure, a genuinely skilled glassblower in his own right, with a fine hand for shape and a reputation, before this particular obsession took hold of him, for clean and reliable work in ordinary greens and ambers that sold consistently well throughout the quarter.

For nearly four years, Kester spent every spare hour of his working life not refining the greens and ambers that had built his actual reputation, but experimenting with mineral combinations meant to reproduce Isbet's blue, buying costly imported cobalt in quantities he could not always justify, ruining batch after batch in pursuit of a shade whose true composition he had never been told, and was, in a strict sense, guessing at from memory and envy rather than any real information.

I watched some of this happen firsthand, because Kester brought a good many of his failed batches to the Long Kiln anyway, out of habit or hope, and I annealed pieces for him across those years that came out of the cooling not blue at all but a muddy, uneven gray-green that satisfied no one, least of all Kester himself, who took to standing over the kiln's small viewing window during the cooling hours in a way I had rarely seen even the most anxious young apprentices do, as though watching harder might somehow change what the mineral mixture inside had already decided to become. I asked him once, gently, why he did not simply go to Isbet directly and ask. He looked at me the way a much younger man looks at an older one who has just suggested something obviously, embarrassingly simple. "Because then it would be her blue I finally made," he said, "not mine." I did not fully understand what he meant by this at the time, and I am not certain, even now, that he understood it either, beyond some private sense that arriving at the answer alone would mean something the answer itself, handed to him, never could.

His wife, Ferra, whom I came to know only slightly better through those years than I knew Kester himself, told me once, in the resigned tone of a woman who has said the same thing to her husband more than once without effect, that she had stopped asking him each evening whether the day's batch had worked, because the answer was so reliably no that the asking itself had become its own small cruelty. "He comes home smelling of burnt cobalt and disappointment in roughly equal measure," she said, "and I have started to wonder whether he would know what to do with himself if he ever actually succeeded, since succeeding was never really the plan he'd built his days around. The batches were the plan. The blue was just the excuse for them."

He did not neglect his ordinary work entirely — he could not have afforded to, and continued to sell his greens and ambers throughout those four years — but the quality of his attention to them thinned noticeably, the way attention always thins when it is being spent somewhere else at the same time, and more than one regular buyer in the quarter mentioned to me, in passing, over those years, that Kester's work seemed to have grown a little careless, a little rushed, without any of them being able to say exactly why.

What Kester never seemed to fully grasp, watching Isbet's workshop from two doors down with an attention that had curdled somewhere along the way from admiration into something closer to grievance, was that the blue itself was not actually the whole of what made Isbet's work valuable. It was the visible symbol of something much less imitable underneath it: fifteen years of patient, unglamorous experiment, most of it invisible, most of it unsuccessful in its moment, that had built in Isbet not just one blue mixture but an entire practical understanding of how minerals behaved in her particular furnace, at her particular heat, with her particular hand — an understanding that could not be reverse-engineered from the outside by anyone trying to guess at a single finished result.

Isbet herself, when I once mentioned Kester's efforts to her, seemed genuinely more puzzled than flattered by them. "He could ask me," she said. "I would not hand him the whole of it — some things a person has to earn through their own failed batches, the way I did — but I would tell him more than he could ever guess correctly on his own. I think he does not want the answer nearly as much as he wants to have arrived at it the same way I did, alone, and that is a much harder thing to hand a person than a mineral list."

I asked Isbet once, in those same years, whether it ever troubled her to watch a fellow glassblower burning through his savings on cobalt trying to reverse-engineer something she would have simply given him for the asking. She thought about the question longer than I expected. "It troubled me less than you'd think," she said finally, "because I remembered my own fourteenth year clearly enough to recognize what he was actually doing, even if he couldn't see it himself. I did the same thing once, chasing a green that a glassblower two towns over kept to herself. I spent a year and a half of my own savings on it before I finally understood that the green wasn't the point — I simply wanted to know I could match anyone, and had picked her particular green as the proof of it, the way Kester picked my blue. I gave it up, eventually, and went back to what became this blue instead, and I have sometimes wondered whether Kester needed his four years the same way I needed my year and a half — not to learn the mineral, but to learn that chasing someone else's answer was never going to feel like the thing he actually wanted, even if he'd gotten it exactly right."

In the fifth year, Kester finally did ask her directly, worn down at last by four years of expensive failure, and Isbet told him plainly and without any particular ceremony roughly what he needed to know — not the exact proportions, which she genuinely could not have given him precisely even had she wanted to, but the general family of minerals involved and the rough range of heat that mattered most. It took him another full year of his own experiment, guided now rather than guessing blind, before he produced a blue of his own — not identical to Isbet's, closer in the end to a deep sea-green than a true blue, but distinctive, sellable, and entirely his, arrived at finally through his own hands rather than hers.

He told me once, years afterward, that the blue he eventually made was, if he was honest, less remarkable than the greens and ambers he had been making before he ever started chasing Isbet's flame, and that he sometimes wondered what those five years might have produced if he had spent them instead simply going deeper into the color he already knew, the way Isbet had gone deeper into hers. "I don't regret learning what I learned," he said. "I regret how long it took me to understand that I was chasing her result instead of doing what she'd actually done, which was spend fifteen years failing at something nobody had told her the answer to. There is no shortcut to that part. I just wasted a few years discovering there wasn't one."

Kester's household, in the years following his own eventual success with the sea-green he finally made his own, settled into a kind of quiet stability his earlier obsessive years had never allowed, and his daughter, apprenticed eventually to his own workshop, told me once that she had grown up on a version of the story considerably softened from the one I've set down here — her father's telling emphasized the discovery rather than the four wasted years, in the way parents often smooth their own histories for their children's benefit. I did not correct her account when she told it to me. I think there is a kind of mercy in letting a person tell their own hard years as a shorter story than they actually lived, so long as they have genuinely learned what the longer version had to teach.

What struck me most, hearing him say this, was how closely it echoed something Isbet herself had told me long before, about her own chase after the green she never caught. She said she had come to think of the four wasted years, in Kester's case, not as pure loss but as a particular kind of tuition that the trade seemed to charge nearly everyone at some point, in one form or another — a fee paid not for the knowledge itself, which could often be gotten far more cheaply simply by asking, but for the harder and more private lesson underneath it, which was that the wanting had never really been about the color at all. "I think every glassblower in this quarter pays that fee once," she told me. "The lucky ones pay it early and cheaply, chasing something small. Kester's misfortune was that his fee came due on something as costly as cobalt, and took him five years instead of one to finish paying."

Envy of a rival's technique mistakes the visible outcome for the invisible method, and spends years trying to reproduce the first without ever doing the second. The color on the shelf is not the craft. The craft is the decade and a half of ruined batches nobody saw, and there has never yet been a way to buy, borrow, or guess your way past that part.

…she genuinely was more concerned with the difficulty of articulating the process than guarding it.

The swan was more than just a flawless creation; it exposed the precariousness of Davor Quill's success, and how easily ambition could be both his salvation and ruin.

IV. The One Swan

Don't mistake artistry for magic. Behind every breathtaking piece of glass is a relentless discipline, a quiet calculation, and an understanding of forces most people never see.

What she'd actually commissioned, that autumn, was a wager the whole harbor town understood immediately: whoever could produce a life-sized bird in glass so white and fine it looked like frozen sea-foam would own not just the considerable fee but the reputation that followed it. The kind of reputation that stuck.

Davor was thirty-one. Gifted. Hungry in the particular way of a man who'd spent a decade being told he was nearly ready for something large without ever quite being handed it.

I remember the afternoon Guen Pell's steward first brought the full commission terms to the Cinderquay, stopping at nearly every workshop along the way. Isbet Voll declined outright, telling the steward that a piece of that scale and risk didn't suit the steady kind of trade she'd built her name on. Marl Ashen, the fishing-float maker whose fuller story appears later in this book, laughed outright and said he wouldn't know where to begin with a swan the size of a grown man.

It was Davor, among nearly a dozen workshops the steward visited that single afternoon, who seemed to hear the commission not as a risk to be weighed but as an invitation he'd been waiting years for someone to extend.

He gave the commission everything. For the better part of a year, he all but abandoned the ordinary trade that had kept his workshop modestly but reliably afloat—the everyday cups, bowls, window panes—in order to devote his furnace time, his materials, and increasingly his household's remaining savings to a single enormous piece that could fail at any one of a hundred stages.

But what was he actually building? He thought he was building his reputation. A cornerstone commission that would establish him among the top rank of Ashmere's glassblowers. And he was building that, in a sense. But he was also building something else entirely—something that looked like an investment in his future but functioned more like a beautiful, fragile monument to a single moment of ambition that had no particular interest in repeating itself.

The swan's neck alone required nine separate attempts before Davor judged the curve worthy of joining to the body at all. Each attempt was a full morning's work undone by evening for a flaw invisible to anyone but him. One of the two assistants Davor hired specifically for the commission told me later that he'd watched Davor stand in front of the seventh attempt for nearly an hour, silent, before finally taking it back to the furnace to melt down and start again. The assistant had asked what was wrong with it. Davor said the curve was perfect everywhere except the last three inches before it would meet the body, and those three inches would bother him every time he looked at it for the rest of his life if he let them stay.

The wings came harder. Built in sections, fused with heat control so exacting that a single ill-timed gust through the workshop's open door cost him four days of joined work in the time it takes a candle to gutter.

I remember Davor arriving at the Long Kiln one evening that particular week looking genuinely uncertain of himself for the first time since I'd known him. He asked whether I thought a piece of that ambition was even possible for a man of his skill, or whether he'd simply mistaken a fine trial swan the size of a hand for evidence he could scale the same delicacy up to something the size of an actual bird.

I told him I didn't know. I'd never watched anyone attempt anything quite like it.

He wasn't foolish. He understood the risks better than anyone outside the trade could. He took every precaution his skill allowed. But glass at that scale carries a kind of risk that patience and skill can reduce without ever eliminating.

The first failure came at the joining of the neck to the body. Davor had rehearsed the join a dozen times in miniature but had never attempted it at full scale, and the piece cracked cleanly across the seam within the Long Kiln's first day of cooling. I opened the door to check on it and found the two halves lying apart. Davor didn't speak for a long while after I showed him. He just stood there looking at the pieces, turned one of them over once in his hands, then set it down and asked—in a voice notably steadier than I expected—when I thought the kiln might next have room for a second attempt.

The second failure, months later, was subtler and in some ways harder to bear. A piece that survived the joining and the full cooling intact, only for Davor to notice, in ordinary daylight rather than the flattering lamplight of his workshop, a faint asymmetry in the wings. No one else in the quarter would likely have caught it. But he refused to let it leave his workshop once he'd seen it, breaking it down for remelting himself rather than risk delivering anything less than what he'd promised Guen Pell in his own mind, whether or not she would ever have known the difference.

Here's what it cost him, that year: regular buyers who'd once come to him reliably for cups and bowls found that his workshop had little ordinary stock on hand and, more than once, no patience to spare for a small order when a swan's wing was cooling in the furnace room behind him. Some of them found other workshops. Not all of them came back.

That erosion was slow enough, and quiet enough, that Davor barely noticed it happening. When you're standing in front of a furnace at dawn trying to judge whether the heat on a swan's wing joint is even enough to hold, you don't think much about the bowl order you turned away three weeks ago. Those feel like reasonable sacrifices. Temporary ones.

The third attempt succeeded.

I was there the night it finally came out of the Long Kiln whole, because Davor asked me to sit with him through the last hours of its cooling. I remember him standing at the small viewing window for the better part of that final night, saying almost nothing, occasionally pressing two fingers flat against the stone as though he could feel through it whether the glass inside was cooling evenly. When I finally opened the door at dawn and lifted the swan free myself—my own hands shaking rather more than they usually did for a piece of that size—Davor didn't reach for it right away. He stood back and looked at it for what felt like a very long moment, the way a man looks at something he's wanted so completely for so long that its actual arrival takes him a while to recognize as real.

"I kept expecting to feel triumphant," he told me afterward. "Mostly what I felt that morning was just relieved it was over."

It was the single finest piece of glasswork I saw in forty years at that fire. A swan so pale and so precisely wrought that it seemed to hold the harbor's own light inside it rather than merely reflect it. When it was displayed at the Founders' Feast, guests who'd come expecting an ordinary centerpiece fell quiet as they approached it. Corliss Fen told me later that Guen Pell herself said very little that evening, choosing instead to stand near the plinth for most of the night, watching her guests' faces as they first caught sight of it—which several people who knew her well took as the clearest sign of satisfaction she was ever likely to give.

Davor's name, for a season, was spoken across Ashmere the way certain rare and beautiful things are spoken of when they first appear and no one's quite gotten used to them yet.

But what had he actually won?

In the two years that followed his triumph, Davor discovered something the applause at the feast hadn't prepared him for: a single spectacular commission, however celebrated, is not a trade. It doesn't repeat itself on demand. It doesn't, by itself, replace the steady custom that had quietly drained away from his workshop during the year he spent building it.

He found himself famous and nearly broke at the same time.

His savings had been spent on materials and furnace time that Guen's generous fee had only partly recovered. His ordinary trade was now scattered among rivals who'd happily absorbed the custom he'd let go. And the swan's fame didn't bring those customers back. It brought admirers. People who wanted to tell him how moved they'd been by the piece at the feast. People who asked, occasionally, whether he might consider attempting another commission of similar ambition, though when he named a price that would actually cover the risk and materials, most of them thanked him politely and never followed up.

He'd proven he could build a spectacular thing under very particular circumstances—one wealthy patron, one specific commission, a year of single-minded focus—but that proof didn't translate into a system he could run twice, or ten times, or build a sustainable practice around. The swan wasn't a template. It was a singularity.

The two lean years that followed were harder, in their quiet way, than the year of building the swan had been, because they lacked even the animating hope that had carried him through the earlier difficulty. He sold a good deal of the fine glass stock he'd accumulated in better years, at prices that gave him little satisfaction. He took on, for the first time since his apprenticeship, small repair commissions he would once have considered beneath him—a cracked window pane here, a rehung shop sign there—simply to keep his household fed while his ordinary custom slowly, painfully found its way back to him.

More than one former customer, drifting back after a year or two with a rival workshop, offered some version of the same apology: they'd assumed, seeing the swan's fame, that Davor's workshop had grown too grand and too busy for their ordinary trade. They'd gone elsewhere without ever thinking to ask.

That's the cost most people miss when they think about chasing a defining piece of work. Not the risk that it fails—Davor's didn't, his swan succeeded spectacularly—but the risk that it succeeds in exactly the way you hoped while quietly hollowing out everything else you'd built your life on. You look up two years later and you're famous for one thing, admired for it, occasionally stopped in the market by someone who wants to tell you how much it meant to them—and you're eating worse than you were before you started because the daily work that actually kept you fed is gone and the spectacular thing that replaced it in your attention turns out not to have any interest in feeding you twice.

Davor rebuilt, in time, and rebuilt well. I saw him some years later running a workshop as steady and reliable as any in the quarter, though he never again attempted a piece on the scale of the swan. I asked him once, in his later years, whether he regretted it.

"No," he said, without much hesitation. "I'd build the swan again tomorrow if Guen Pell walked back through my door. What I wouldn't do again is let it eat the rest of my trade while I built it. I know now those were two separate risks, and I only ever meant to take the first one."

The risk of attempting something ambitious is not the same as the risk of letting that attempt consume everything else you've built. You can take the first risk without taking the second. But you have to see them as separate decisions, and most of us don't, because the ambitious thing is so loud and bright and demanding when it's in front of us that the quiet daily work we're neglecting doesn't start screaming until it's already half-gone.

So here's what I'd want you to take from Davor's story: ask yourself, right now, before you're six months in and too committed to back out—what does this actually require me to stop doing? Not what will I pause temporarily, because "temporary" has a way of stretching longer than you think. What will I genuinely have to stop, or let go, or watch drift away to someone else? Write that list down. Look at it. Then ask whether you can afford to lose those things even if the big project succeeds exactly the way you're hoping it will.

Because the real gamble Davor took—the one he didn't fully see until it was already made—wasn't whether the swan would work. It was whether he could afford to be the man who'd built it. And the answer, for two lean years afterward, was no. Not yet. Not without rebuilding, from scratch, the foundation he'd let crumble while he was reaching for something higher.

The swan made Davor Quill's name. The daily work he'd neglected would have let him enjoy having it. Most of us, when we're standing where he stood that autumn afternoon with Guen Pell's commission in hand, don't think to check whether we're holding both.

Odalys built her business on price, but Corliss Fen understood that true value wasn't simply about affordability – it was about weathering storms with quiet dignity.

V. The Apprentice's Fair Price

The chipped ceramic mug warmed my hands as I watched Old Man Tiber meticulously arrange sea-worn stones outside his curio shop—a precarious balance that mirrored the lives of those who worked along the Cinderquay.

She had apprenticed under a master named Fenna Cray, a competent but famously stern woman who had, by Odalys's own account, not once in four years told her apprentice that a piece was good enough without immediately naming three ways it could have been better, and Odalys told me once that she suspected her later trouble with pricing had its roots in that apprenticeship more than in any pure calculation about the market — a lingering, unexamined sense that her own work could never quite be worth what an established master's work was worth, learned so early and so thoroughly that it took her three exhausting years in her own stall to even notice the belief was there, let alone question whether it was true.

For a time, this worked exactly as she had hoped. Buyers who might otherwise have gone to an established workshop out of habit tried Odalys instead, drawn by prices that made an ordinary cup or bowl feel almost like a bargain, and for two years her custom grew steadily on the strength of it. She told herself, during those years, that she was simply building a reputation the honest way — through volume and goodwill rather than through the kind of established-name premium that older workshops charged almost as a matter of course.

What Odalys had not fully accounted for was what her pricing was actually costing her, beneath the visible growth of her custom. Fine sand, good mineral color, dry seasoned wood for the furnace —

none of these came cheaply, and a price set low enough to undercut established masters left her, once those costs were paid, with a margin so thin that she could not set anything meaningful aside, could not afford to let a furnace run half-empty while she experimented with anything beyond her safest, most reliable pieces, and could not, when a bad batch of sand or an unlucky run of cracked pieces struck her workshop, absorb the loss the way a workshop with a healthier margin could.

I kept, as I always did, a rough sense of who along the harbor road was bringing steady custom to the Long Kiln and who wasn't, and I noticed, well before Odalys herself seemed to, that her deliveries had grown both more frequent and more modest — smaller batches, brought more often, as though she could no longer afford to let a week's work accumulate before needing the coin it would bring in. I mentioned this once to her, gently, expecting perhaps that she would tell me business was simply brisk. Instead she admitted, with a tiredness that surprised me in someone still so young, that she had begun timing her deliveries around which household debts were coming due that particular week, selling whatever was nearest finished rather than whatever might have benefited from another day's careful work, because the coin from Tuesday's pieces was already spoken for by Thursday's woodcutter.

She told me, too, of a particular evening that stayed with her long afterward, when a fine bowl she had shaped with real care — the kind of piece she might, at a fairer price, have been proud to let sit a season longer before finding exactly the right buyer for it — went instead to the first customer who offered anything close to her asking price, a merchant's steward who haggled her down further still before she agreed, simply because she needed the coin that same evening to cover her wood delivery. "I remember watching him carry it out the door," she said, "and thinking that I had made something genuinely good, and sold it like something merely adequate, because adequate was what I could afford to have made that week."

By her third year, Odalys was, by any honest accounting, busier than almost any glassblower her age in the Cinderquay and considerably poorer than her volume of custom would have suggested to anyone glancing at her order book rather than her actual accounts. She worked longer hours than the established masters around her, for less real return, and had begun, without quite admitting it to herself, to resent the very customers whose loyalty she had worked so hard to win, because each new order felt less like an opportunity and more like another set of hours she could not really afford to give away at the price she had set for them.

It was Isbet Voll — whose own blue, by then, needed no undercutting to draw custom — who finally said something to her directly, having watched the pattern from a few doors down for long enough to recognize where it was heading. "You are not competing with me on price," Isbet told her, one evening when Odalys had stayed unusually late at her furnace, exhausted in a way that had become ordinary for her rather than occasional. "You are competing with your own sand merchant and your own woodcutter, and you are losing to both of them every single day, because you have priced your hours at less than it costs you to work them."

Odalys resisted the advice for longer than she later admitted was wise, telling herself that raising her prices would undo the very custom she had spent three years building. She confided to me, during that resistant stretch, a fear that struck me as entirely genuine even if it later proved unfounded: that she had built her whole young reputation on being the affordable choice, and that a workshop known for one thing could not simply announce itself to be known for something else without losing the very identity that had drawn its first customers through the door at all. "I am not Isbet Voll," she said. "Nobody crosses the quarter for my name alone. They cross it for my prices, and if I take the prices away, I am afraid there will be nothing left underneath them that anyone actually wanted."

When she finally did raise them — cautiously, in modest steps rather than all at once, over the better part of a year — she lost, as she had feared, some portion of the buyers who had come to her specifically for the bargain rather than for the work itself. But she found, to her genuine surprise, that most of her real custom stayed, because it had never actually been the price that kept them coming back, whatever she had assumed; it had been the quality of the work itself, which had been there all along, simply priced too low for her to properly sustain it.

The first customer to leave her over the new prices was a household steward who had been among her most frequent early buyers, and who told her plainly, on his way out the door for what both of them understood would be the last time, that he had always assumed her low prices meant she simply valued custom over coin, and that raising them now felt to him like a kind of quiet insult to the loyalty he'd shown her those first years. Odalys told me this exchange had cost her more sleep than almost anything else in the adjustment, not because she doubted her decision but because she genuinely liked the man and hated that he'd left believing something about her that wasn't true. She did not chase him to explain further. She simply let him go, the way she had learned, slowly, that a fair price sometimes cost her exactly the customers who had most benefited from the unfair one.

Within two years of the adjustment, Odalys was earning, on considerably less volume, a genuinely comfortable living for the first time since opening her stall, with margin enough, finally, to set aside good sand for experiments, to let a furnace run a little under capacity when a piece needed extra care, and to weather, without real crisis, a bad batch when one eventually came. She told me once, looking back on those early years, that she had mistaken being busy for being valued, and had needed three exhausting years to understand that the two were not, in fact, the same thing at all.

She took, in her later years, to mentoring young apprentices finishing their own training, and made a point, every single time, of walking each of them through her own early accounts — the real numbers, sand costs against sale prices, laid out plainly rather than glossed over the way an older master's pride might have tempted her to gloss them. "I could tell you simply to charge fairly," she told one apprentice, in an exchange the young woman later repeated to me nearly word for word. "But 'charge fairly' means nothing until you've actually written down what an hour of your own work costs you to give away, in wood and sand and the roof over your own furnace. I did not do that math honestly until my fourth year. I want you to do it in your first."

"I thought I was being generous to my customers," she said. "I was actually being dishonest with myself about what my own hours were worth, and calling the dishonesty generosity because it felt kinder to describe it that way."

Underselling a craft rarely feels, in the moment, like a mistake. It feels like humility, or generosity, or simple good sense in the face of established competition. But a price that does not cover what the work genuinely costs — in materials, in hours, in the margin a person needs to survive their own bad seasons — is not a gift to the customer. It is a debt quietly transferred onto the craftsman's own future, due whether or not she has noticed yet that she is paying it.

Fenna Cray, Odalys's own stern old master, lived long enough to watch her former apprentice's eventual recovery, and told me once, in her own final years, that she recognized more of herself in Odalys's early undervaluing than she had ever admitted to the girl directly while she was still teaching her. "I priced my own work too cheaply for the better part of a decade, when I was young," she said, to my genuine surprise, since nothing in her later reputation suggested any such history. "I never told any of my apprentices that, Odalys included, because I thought a master was supposed to appear to have always known better. I think now that was its own kind of dishonesty, dressed up as good example-setting, and I have wondered since whether Odalys might have found her way to fair pricing a year or two sooner if I had simply told her the truth about my own foolish twenties instead of pretending I'd never had any."

The borrowed furnace represented a lifeline for some, but the gilded window signaled an instability in Davor's work which would soon threaten everything he had built.

VI. The Borrowed Furnace

The chipped ceramic mug warmed my hands, even through the thick wool gloves. December in the Cinderquay wasn't a cold that stole your breath so much as one that seeped into your bones and lingered.

It was a far cry from the grand display he'd once commanded on Harbor Road.

Old Man Hemlock, perpetually draped in nets and smelling faintly of brine, leaned against my elbow. "See him?" he grunted, nodding towards Corliss with a stubby finger. "Used to be royalty, that one. Lit up the whole quarter. Now… just makes glasses." He didn't say it with malice. More with the pragmatic acceptance of someone who'd seen enough seasons turn in Ashmere to know how quickly fortunes could shift.

"He always did have a good eye," I said, taking a sip of my lukewarm tea.

Hemlock snorted. "An eye for presentation, maybe. Not necessarily for… foundations." He paused, then lowered his voice conspiratorially. "Borrowed furnace, that workshop was. Built on air and someone else's patience."

I knew the story. I had documented enough collapses over my years at the Long Kiln to recognize the pattern before it fully bloomed. But watching Corliss now, hands moving with practiced precision, I wondered—how many passersby ever connected this quiet craftsman to the man whose showroom had once drawn customers from across the harbor road? How many saw only the present and not the ghost of what had been?

Here's what I've learned: most businesses don't fail from bad luck, or poor timing, or even lack of talent. They fail because the person at the helm can't reliably tell the difference between an investment that builds lasting strength and an expense that merely *looks* like it does. And by the time they learn to distinguish them, the money's gone.

Think of a shipwright building a vessel. He invests in seasoned oak for the keel – expensive, difficult to work, but the thing that keeps the ship from breaking apart in a storm. That's real. Or he splurges on gilded carvings and brightly colored sails, hoping flash and spectacle will attract buyers. Both add cost. Only one adds value. But which one looks better in the harbor at dawn, when potential buyers are walking past?

That's the question, isn't it? Not which choice is *right*, but which one *feels* right when you're standing there with the money in your hand and a dozen voices in your head telling you what success is supposed to look like.

Corliss Fen hadn't lacked talent. Even now, his glasswork was consistently admired. He understood the subtleties of color, the delicate dance between heat and pressure, the precise moment to withdraw a piece from the flame before it sagged into ruin. But six years before everything came undone, he'd started borrowing. Not for supplies. Not for innovation. For *image*.

A wider showroom first. Then better lighting—those amber-paned windows that caught the afternoon sun and made everything inside glow like treasure. Then an exclusive annealing furnace that freed him from the shared schedule at the Long Kiln, where the rest of us had to book time slots and wait our turn like everyone else. Each improvement was presented to himself—and subtly, to his growing clientele—as a natural progression. A necessary step towards greater prosperity.

He wasn't accruing debt. He was "investing in growth."

But was he? Or was he funding a facade, building a beautiful room designed to make ordinary goods appear extraordinary, without ever pausing to consider what that room itself was costing him?

I remember the first time I walked into that showroom after the renovations. It took my breath away, I'll admit it. The light came through those amber panes and turned everything golden. Even simple water glasses looked like something a duke might drink from. Corliss stood there beaming, one hand resting on the edge of a display table he'd commissioned from a carpenter in the next district—solid walnut, dovetailed corners, the kind of craftsmanship that whispered *permanence*. "What do you think?" he'd asked me, and I'd said what anyone would say: "It's beautiful."

What I didn't say—what I didn't even fully understand yet—was that beauty and strength aren't the same thing. One can exist without the other. And in business, choosing beauty over strength is a bargain with a very specific expiration date.

His eldest daughter, Elara, told me about the evenings he spent poring over his accounts by lamplight after that first year in the new space. A careful quiet descended upon the household whenever a letter arrived bearing the seal of Brannic Tor, the river town lender. Not fear, she'd said. Tension. A premonition hanging in the air. She hadn't understood it then, not fully. She was fourteen. But I understood it the moment she described the way her father's shoulders would tighten, the way his smile would flicker and resettle whenever someone complimented the showroom.

He was walking on unstable ground. And he knew it.

But here's the thing about unstable ground: you can walk on it for a surprisingly long time if you're careful about where you put your weight. Corliss was very, very careful. He juggled payments, timed his orders, made sure there was always just enough coming in to keep Brannic Tor patient. For three years, it worked. The showroom drew customers. The customers brought revenue. The revenue kept the whole structure from collapsing.

Then came the season he could have escaped.

A strong run of orders—commissions from two merchant families preparing for weddings, a bulk order of wine goblets from a tavern owner expanding into three new locations—left him with enough surplus to make a significant payment on the debt. Maybe even clear half of it. He sat with his account books that evening, he told me later, seriously considering it. The numbers were right there in front of him. He could *see* the path out.

But then he decided instead to put the money towards another addition to the showroom. A separate alcove for displaying his finest pieces, with its own dedicated lighting and a small bench where customers could sit and examine the glasswork up close. "I told myself the alcove would earn back its own cost within a year," he said to me months after everything fell apart, his voice flat with the particular exhaustion that comes from hindsight. "And it did, in a narrow sense. But that was the season I could have started climbing out, and I chose instead to build one story higher."

Why? Why would a man who *knew* he was in danger choose to go deeper instead of pulling back?

I've thought about that question for years. Not just about Corliss, but about every craftsman, every merchant, every builder I've watched make the same choice. And here's what I think: he couldn't see the line anymore between building something real and creating an illusion. The showroom had *become* the business in his mind. Improving it felt like improving the work itself. And maybe more than that—maybe he'd started to believe his own performance. Maybe walking into that golden-lit room every morning and seeing customers' faces light up had convinced him that success was already here, that he'd already *made* it, and all he needed to do was keep polishing the frame.

That's the trick of borrowed prosperity. It doesn't feel borrowed. It feels *earned.*

By his fifth year in that showroom, Corliss wasn't borrowing to expand anymore. He was borrowing to maintain the appearance of expansion. The amber windows needed constant cleaning—salt air from the harbor etched the glass, and anything less than perfect clarity ruined the effect. The walnut display tables required regular oiling. The exclusive furnace demanded more fuel than a shared kiln ever would have, because it ran on his schedule, not an efficient rotation. The very image that had attracted customers now required continuous investment just to *stay* attractive.

He'd built a gilded cage. And every month, the bars grew a little tighter.

I wasn't there the morning the letter arrived, but Elara described it to me in detail years later, when she was old enough to understand what she'd witnessed. Brannic Tor had died of a fever. His holdings had passed to a nephew—a man from the southern coastal cities who had none of his uncle's patience for "informal upriver arrangements."

The nephew wanted full payment within a single season.

Corliss had been standing at the kitchen table when he read it. Elara said he didn't shout. Didn't rage. Didn't crumple the paper or throw it across the room. He just… stilled. Something in his face went cold, as if all the warmth had been extinguished. He folded the letter carefully, almost reverently, and said to no one in particular, "I always knew this could happen. I simply never let myself believe it actually would."

He couldn't pay. The showroom, the furnace, the golden-lit alcove—none of it had generated enough *actual* profit to cover what he owed. And because the debt had remained hidden for so long, its sudden exposure looked like a catastrophic failure instead of an unfortunate circumstance. Word spread fast in a district like Cinderquay. By the end of the week, creditors who'd been perfectly content to wait for payment were suddenly demanding it immediately, afraid they'd be last in line when the workshop was liquidated.

The showroom's amber-paned windows were among the first things sold. The fishmonger next door bought them at a steep discount, thinking he might use them somehow, then passed them on to a builder two towns over when he realized he had no use for decorative glass. It was a scene I'd witnessed before, in different cities, with different merchants. Each time, it struck me as a particularly bitter irony: something created to *enhance* value being reduced to its base components, stripped of all pretense, worth only what someone would pay for the raw materials.

And yet beneath the wreckage, Corliss himself hadn't changed. He was still the same careful craftsman who had once refused to rush eight goblets out of an oven because the annealing wasn't quite right, who could look at a piece of glass and tell you whether it would hold or shatter just by the way the light moved through it. But he had allowed the *frame* around that craft—the showroom, the debt, the image—to grow beyond what the work itself could sustain. He'd trusted for six years that next season's profit would catch up to this season's expense.

A trust betrayed by a stranger's death and a nephew's cold arithmetic.

He rebuilt, eventually. A small stall near the wharf, tucked between the fishmongers and a woman who sold woven baskets. No glass panes. No grand display. Just simple work done with quiet competence. I asked him once, about a year after he'd set up there, if he ever thought about the showroom.

"Every day," he said. He was shaping a water glass as he spoke, his hands moving with the same practiced rhythm they always had. "Not with longing, if that's what you're asking. With a kind of relief, mostly, that I no longer have to keep a room like that lit and dusted and *believed in*."

He paused, testing the weight of the glass in his palm, then set it carefully on the rack to cool.

"I make less now than I did in the years the showroom stood," he said. "I sleep better than I did in any of them."

The truth is, debt itself isn't the enemy in a craft like glassblowing—or any trade, for that matter. Nearly every workshop in Ashmere has borrowed at some point. The danger isn't in the borrowing. It's in the *concealing*. In dressing it up in fine panes and good light so that everyone extending you further trust—customers, suppliers, lenders—is doing so on a false premise.

A furnace built on ground that isn't there burns just as bright as one built on solid stone. Right up until the ground gives way.

I think often of Old Man Hemlock, down by the salt marshes, though he's been dead now for fifteen years. He wasn't a glassblower—he was a shipwright, and for thirty years he built sturdy little fishing skiffs. Nothing fancy. No elaborate carvings or painted hulls. Just solid boats that wouldn't split apart in a chop. He always paid cash for his timber, even when it meant waiting an extra season to get the best price. "A man can rebuild a boat from splinters," he used to say, and I remember it clearly because he said it with such quiet conviction, standing in his workshop with wood shavings stuck to his beard. "But he can't rebuild trust once it's broken."

He wasn't talking about carpentry. He was talking about the slow accumulation of reputation, the kind that lets you borrow against tomorrow without ever needing to ask.

Corliss Fen hadn't understood that lesson. Or maybe he had, and simply convinced himself he was an exception to it. That his skill, his eye for light, his sheer *talent* would somehow be enough to hold everything aloft, even when the foundations were sand. It's a story I've seen repeated more times than I care to count. The artist who believes artistry absolves him from arithmetic. The merchant who confuses charisma with capital.

The irony—and I mean this, it's kept me awake more nights than I'd like to admit—is that Corliss's downfall could have been avoided with one simple act. Transparency. Had he gone to Brannic Tor in that third year, when the surplus came in, and said, "Times are tight, I need an extension," he might still be working in that showroom today. Maybe with a revised payment plan. Maybe with a partner brought in to share the risk. But still *there*, still building, still growing.

But pride, or perhaps a desperate fear of losing face, kept him trapped. He believed that admitting weakness would be more damaging than concealing it.

A calculation that proved tragically wrong.

I've seen younger artisans at the Long Kiln make versions of the same mistake. They take on an ambitious commission, overextend themselves, then refuse to ask for help because they're afraid of looking incompetent. So they work late into the night, sacrificing quality, sacrificing sleep, sacrificing their own clarity of mind, all in the name of maintaining a facade of control. And inevitably, something cracks. Literally, sometimes, if we're talking about glass.

The lesson isn't that you should always reveal your vulnerabilities. There are times when discretion is essential, when showing your hand too early costs you the deal or the commission or the respect you've worked years to build. I'm not naive about that. But there's a difference—a critical difference—between strategic silence and deliberate deception. The former protects what you've built. The latter just delays the inevitable collapse. And the longer you delay it, the more devastating it becomes.

My own workshop, the Long Kiln, was never lavish. It wasn't ugly, but it wasn't trying to be anything other than what it was: a functional space where serious work got done. We didn't bother with appearances beyond basic cleanliness and order. If we couldn't deliver something by a certain date, we said so. If we needed help—an extra pair of hands, a borrowed tool, advice on a technique we hadn't mastered—we asked for it. It wasn't glamorous. But it worked. Because at the end of the day, trust is worth more than any amount of amber-tinted glass.

Corliss, after his fall, didn't become bitter. He didn't blame Brannic Tor's nephew, or the creditors, or the fickle customers who'd stopped coming once the showroom closed. He simply accepted that he had made a series of choices, and those choices had led him here, and no amount of anger or regret would change the ledger. It was a quiet dignity I admired, even as I grieved the loss of what he could have been—not just a skilled craftsman, but a *great* one, the kind whose name carries weight for generations.

He rebuilt his trade slowly. One piece at a time. He didn't try to recreate the grandeur. Didn't chase accolades. Just focused on making good glass—honest glass—and letting it speak for itself. And in doing so, I think he found something that had eluded him during all those years of striving and concealing: a kind of peace.

I bought a bowl from him a few weeks before I retired from the Long Kiln. Small, simple, perfectly formed. I didn't need it—I had more bowls than I knew what to do with—but I wanted to support him. And I wanted a reminder.

Of what happens when the ground you're standing on is real. And what happens when it's not.

Now here's the part I need you to sit with, because I've been talking about Corliss this whole time but I'm not really talking about Corliss, am I? I'm talking about the thing you're holding together right now with borrowed time. Not necessarily money, though it often is. Maybe it's a reputation you've stretched just a little too far. A relationship built on assumptions you've never voiced. A version of yourself you're performing because the real version doesn't look successful enough.

What happens when the letter arrives? When the nephew calls in the debt? When someone asks a direct question and suddenly the ground you've been walking on isn't there anymore?

Don't wait for that moment. Because it always, *always* arrives. The only choice you have is whether you'll be standing on stone or standing on air when it does.

I've watched people spend decades maintaining the illusion. Entire careers built on the assumption that no one will look too closely. Marriages where both people are performing different scripts, never quite saying what they mean, never quite asking what they fear to know. Businesses held together by momentum and credit lines and the collective agreement not to examine the foundation too hard.

The exhausting part isn't the performance itself. It's the constant vigilance. The mental accounting. You have to remember what you told whom. You have to track which version of the story you're living in at any given moment. You have to monitor every conversation for the question that might unravel everything.

And here's what no one tells you: the longer you maintain it, the harder it becomes to imagine anything else. The borrowed furnace starts to feel like it was always yours. You forget what it's like to generate your own heat. The performance becomes the only version of yourself you remember how to be.

I knew someone once who spent five years in a job he'd lied his way into. Not a big lie—he'd exaggerated a skill on his resume, claimed fluency he didn't quite have. For the first few months, he lived in terror of being found out. But he was smart, worked hard, learned fast. After a year, he was competent. After two, he was good. After five, he was legitimately excellent at the work.

But he never stopped feeling like a fraud. Never stopped waiting for someone to pull the thread. The fact that he'd become exactly what he'd pretended to be didn't matter. The foundation was still borrowed. The heat was still someone else's.

That's the insidious part. Even when you grow into the role, even when you become the thing you were only performing, if you built it on a lie, you never quite trust it. You never quite live in it. You're always standing guard at the door, waiting for the nephew to arrive.

So what's the alternative?

It's not confession. I'm not suggesting you schedule a meeting Monday morning to announce every half-truth you've ever told. That's not courage—that's just a different kind of performance, the dramatic gesture that lets you feel noble while actually just creating chaos.

The alternative is quieter. It's the decision to stop adding to the pile. To stop taking out new loans against a future you're not sure you can afford. To stop saying yes to things you mean no to. To stop building on sand and calling it bedrock.

It means looking at the borrowed furnace and asking: what would it cost to install my own? Not in some distant, theoretical future. Now. This year. This month.

Maybe it means admitting to someone that you don't know something you've been pretending to understand. Maybe it means having the conversation you've been avoiding because it might mean losing something. Maybe it means walking away from the identity that looks good but doesn't fit, even if you don't yet know what will replace it.

The cost is real. I won't pretend otherwise. When you stop maintaining the illusion, things shift. Some of them fall. Not everything—usually not even most things—but some things will not survive the transition from borrowed heat to your own furnace.

But here's what you get in return: you get to stop being afraid of the mail. You get to stop monitoring every conversation for landmines. You get to live in your own life instead of guarding someone else's story.

You get to build on stone.

A chipped mug and a vanished workshop are haunting reminders of what is lost when markets shift—and Ysolt Kane knew how to see that coming.

VII. The Gilded Window

The storefront was empty, but it wasn't the emptiness of abandonment; it was the starkness of potential—a space where Davor Quill's creations once shone, now echoing with silence.

Or rather, the space *where* Davor Quill's workshop used to be. The glass itself had been removed some months ago, replaced with plain, serviceable wood – a quiet testament to fortunes shifted and tastes grown cold. Still, even stripped bare, the archway held a phantom glow in my memory. It wasn't the craftsmanship I remembered most. It was watching people stop mid-stride to stare at it, their faces doing this complicated dance between admiration and something uglier.

I was waiting for Perrin Sable. He'd sent word yesterday, a terse note delivered by a boy who looked permanently braced against the wind: "Meet me at Tiber's. Need to talk about windows."

Perrin had always been a man of few words, even when he had something substantial to say. A quiet competence in a trade filled with flamboyant showmanship. But that note felt weighted in a way his usual correspondence didn't. And after years spent observing glassblowers – their ambitions, their insecurities, the fragile balance between artistry and commerce – I'd learned to trust my gut.

He arrived precisely on time, his coat collar turned up against the damp air, a familiar weariness etched around his eyes. No greeting. Just a nod toward Tiber, who promptly slid a second mug across the counter filled with steaming, bitter brew. Perrin took it without a word, and we sat in silence for a long moment, listening to the market clamor.

"So," I said finally. "Windows."

He didn't meet my gaze. His eyes were fixed on a knot of sailors haggling over rope, his fingers tracing the rim of his mug. "It feels ridiculous, saying it aloud."

"Ridiculous how?"

"Like admitting you chased a fool's errand. Like confessing you mistook wanting to *be seen* with wanting something worthwhile." He finally looked up, and his eyes held something close to shame. "I nearly ruined myself over a piece of glass, Eleanor. A beautiful piece, yes, but unnecessary."

Unnecessary was an understatement. Perrin had borrowed heavily against everything he owned – even the small plot of land inherited from his mother – to commission a window that rivaled Davor Quill's famed archway. It hadn't been about improving his craft or expanding his business.

It had been about capturing a feeling. The raw, unexpected envy that gripped him the morning he first stood before Davor's illuminated storefront.

I remembered that morning vividly. I was on my way to settle a kiln dispute between two apprentices when I paused in the square. Not because of the window itself, but because of the crowd it had drawn. They weren't admiring the artistry, not exactly. They were measuring themselves against it. Each face held a quiet calculation, a silent comparison between their own lives and the gleaming spectacle before them.

And Perrin? He'd stood there longer than anyone else, arms crossed tight across his chest, his gaze traveling slowly across every panel of colored glass as if memorizing each hue. I'd seen that look before – in ship captains eyeing a rival vessel's new sails, in merchants coveting a competitor's opulent display. It wasn't admiration. It was hunger. A desperate need to be perceived as something more.

Here's what I've learned after three decades in this trade: most workshops don't collapse because the work is bad. They collapse because someone confused a symbol of success with the substance of it. They see another glassblower's achievement and think, *If I just had that, if I just looked like that, everything would change.* And by the time they realize they've built their entire operation on that flawed premise, they're staring into an abyss of debt with no clear way out.

"You thought it would change things," I said. "The workshop, the customers..."

He snorted softly. "I thought it would change *me*. Make me noticed." He paused, then added with a wry twist of his lips, "As if being noticed is the same as being respected."

"Tell me about the window."

He began slowly, recounting the years leading up to that commission. His early apprenticeship under Wren Calder – a stern but gifted glassblower who'd instilled in him a respect for discipline and craftsmanship. The gradual building of his own workshop, solid and reliable, serving a loyal clientele. A good life by any measure.

But quiet. Unremarkable.

"My brothers," he said, almost as an afterthought. "They were always the ones people talked about. Oldest was a soldier, came back with stories that filled the tavern for weeks. Youngest had a gift for charm. Could sell sand to a desert nomad." He looked down at his hands, calloused and stained with years of working glass. "I was just the quiet one. The worker."

And he'd decided, on that morning in the square, that enough was enough.

The commission took eight months. Perrin had hired Maryl Kess, one of the finest glass artisans on the coast, to design it. Not quite as grand as Davor's – he hadn't possessed the funds for such extravagance – but striking nonetheless. Deep blues bleeding into amber, a pattern of interlocking crescents that caught the afternoon sun and threw golden coins of light across his showroom floor.

For exactly three weeks, it worked.

Customers flocked to his workshop, drawn by the spectacle. They'd stand in his doorway, shading their eyes against the brilliance, and ask to see his finest pieces. He sold more in those three weeks than he had in the previous six months.

But then something shifted. The customers who came for the window weren't the customers who needed what Perrin actually made. They wanted showpieces, conversation starters, objects that screamed *look at me* rather than pieces that served a genuine purpose. And Perrin, caught in the momentum of those early sales, convinced himself he needed to meet that demand.

He started taking commissions he wasn't equipped to handle. Elaborate stemware that required techniques he hadn't fully mastered. Ornamental vessels that demanded materials he couldn't afford. The debts mounted quickly, spiraling out of control as he chased the clientele his window had attracted but his skills couldn't sustain.

"I watched it go," he said, his voice barely above a whisper. "Saw the buyer walking away with my mother's land, knowing I'd gotten less than it was worth. And all I could think about was Davor Quill, standing in front of his window, bathed in morning light."

Let me interrupt myself here to ask you something. Have you ever made a decision – a big one, a costly one – not because it served your actual goals but because you needed someone else to see you making it?

Think about that for a moment. Because the answer matters more than you might realize.

Perrin spent four lean years clawing his way back to solvency. Working longer hours than ever before, taking any commission that came through his door, sacrificing everything to repay his debts. He didn't complain, not once. But I could see the toll it had taken. The quiet competence was still there, but now it was tempered with hard-earned humility.

"Davor Quill," I said, "knew about your window."

Perrin nodded. "He sent word after things had settled somewhat. Said he barely noticed it at the time, too preoccupied with his own troubles." A flicker of amusement crossed his face. "The irony wasn't lost on me."

I thought of Rasmus Ilde, the old shipwright who'd watched this same pattern play out on the docks. He once told me about a captain who'd insisted on adding an extra mast to his vessel simply for the appearance of grandeur. Didn't consider whether it would actually improve performance, whether the hull could handle the additional weight, whether his crew had the skill to manage it. Just wanted to sail into harbor looking like he commanded something impressive.

"The mast always goes up faster than anyone thinks through what it's for," Rasmus had said, shaking his head. "Taking it back down, though? That's when you find out what the ship was actually worth."

The spice stall bell tinkled as Old Man Tiber refilled our mugs. The market continued its relentless rhythm, oblivious to the small drama unfolding behind his counter.

Here's what Perrin figured out during those four years, and what took me far too long to learn in my own practice: there's a test you can run on any investment before you make it. It's simple, brutally so, but most people won't do it because the answer scares them.

Ask yourself: *If no one ever knew about this, would I still want it?*

If the honest answer is no – if the value exists only in being seen having it – you're not making an investment. You're buying a gilded window. And gilded windows don't keep the rain out.

Perrin looked at me directly, his voice clear and steady for the first time that morning. "I don't think I wanted a window. I think I wanted, for once in my life, to be the brother people stopped in the street to talk about. And I picked the nearest available object that seemed like it might buy me that."

He paused.

"Which happened, in that particular season, to be a piece of colored glass."

The late afternoon light slanted across the harbor road as I walked away from our conversation that day. I passed Perrin's workshop – the window long gone, replaced with a simple wooden panel painted muted gray. It looked right. Not grand, not impressive, but solid.

Dependable. A quiet signal that something fundamental had shifted within those walls.

I didn't stop. I kept walking, but my thoughts stayed with that empty frame.

Because here's the part that haunts me: I've done it too. Not with windows, but with other things. A new kiln I didn't need but wanted people to know I could afford. Taking on an apprentice more to prove I'd "made it" than because I had work that required another set of hands. Small decisions, maybe, compared to Perrin's near-ruin. But the mechanism was identical.

The desire to be perceived as successful instead of actually building something that lasts.

So let me give you something concrete to walk away with, something you can do Monday morning when you're back at your desk or your workbench or wherever you make the decisions that shape your life.

Write down the three biggest investments you're considering right now. Could be money, could be time, could be attention. Doesn't matter. Just the three things you're genuinely contemplating putting resources toward.

Now run each one through that test: *If no one ever knew about this, would I still want it?*

Be honest. Savagely honest. Because the investments that survive that question – the ones you'd pursue even in complete obscurity – those are the ones built on substance. Those are the ones that compound. The others? They're gilded windows. Beautiful, expensive, and ultimately hollow.

But here's the harder part, and this is where Perrin's story gets interesting in ways he didn't fully articulate that morning.

It's not enough to simply avoid the gilded window. You have to know what you're building *instead.* Because envy doesn't just destroy by making you chase the wrong things – it destroys by making you forget what the right things were in the first place.

Perrin told me, months later, that the worst part of those four years wasn't the debt or the humiliation. It was the morning he woke up and realized he'd forgotten why he became a glassblower in the first place. The debt he could calculate, could work off piece by piece. But the lost clarity about his own purpose? That took longer to recover.

He'd spent so long measuring himself against Davor Quill's standards that he'd stopped asking what *his* standards even were.

A few weeks after our conversation at Tiber's stall, I received an unexpected visit from Davor himself. He'd heard through the usual harbor-road gossip about my discussions with Perrin and wanted to set the record straight. I found him in his workshop, surrounded by half-finished swans and the acrid smell of molten glass.

"Perrin makes it sound as though I led him astray," Davor said, not unkindly but with a definite edge.

"Did you?"

"I built something beautiful. If that made him feel inadequate, that's hardly my fault."

I took a seat on a stool near his workbench. "You're right. It's not your fault. But tell me something – why did *you* build it?"

He blinked. “The window?”

“Yes.”

“To attract customers. To establish my reputation. To—“

“If no one ever saw it,” I interrupted, “would you have still wanted it?”

The question hung in the air between us. Davor’s hands stilled over the piece he’d been shaping. For a long moment, he didn’t answer.

Then, quietly: “I don’t know.”

That’s the thing about gilded windows. They don’t just trap the people who chase them. They trap the people who build them too.

The harbor road is full of beautiful things – gleaming glass, polished brass, intricately carved wood. But what I’ve learned, what Perrin learned the hard way, what maybe Davor was just beginning to understand that afternoon, is this:

The question isn’t whether you can afford the window.

The question is whether you can afford to spend the next four years – or fourteen, or forty – paying for something that was never really yours to begin with. Something you built not because it served your purpose, but because it served your image of what you thought you were supposed to be.

And the real cost, the one that doesn’t show up in any ledger?

It’s the workshop you didn’t build. The skills you didn’t develop. The genuine work you didn’t do because you were too busy maintaining the illusion.

Perrin's story didn't end with revelation and immediate redemption. Recovery rarely works that way. But it *did* end with a choice he makes every morning now, a discipline he's built from the rubble of that expensive mistake.

Before he takes on any new project, any new commission, any investment of time or money or attention, he asks himself that question. The one that burns away everything false.

If no one ever knew, would I still want this?

And the work that survives that fire? That's what he builds his days around now.

What survives *your* fire?

But even the most unrepeatable piece can't save you from the relentless demands of time, as Sella Marsh discovered while freely sharing her knowledge with anyone who asked.

VIII. The Unrepeatable Piece

I want to return, briefly, to Davor Quill's swan, because the perfection we saw on display hid a desperate gamble beneath its surface.

The swan made Davor's name across Ashmere, and for a year or two afterward, wealthy patrons across the harbor town came to his workshop specifically hoping he could produce something in its spirit — not another swan exactly, but a piece of similar ambition, similar scale, similar astonishment. Davor, chastened by how close the first commission had come to ruining him, declined most of these requests, and the ones he did accept, he priced and paced carefully, never again letting a single piece consume the whole of his workshop's attention the way the swan had.

What he discovered, across those next several years, was a harder truth than the near-ruin the swan itself had cost him: the swan could not actually be repeated, not by design and not by accident, no matter how carefully he tried. He attempted, twice, pieces in a similar spirit — a great glass heron for one patron, a school of glass fish suspended on wire for another — and both were competent, well-received, honestly priced work. Neither one, by Davor's own honest accounting and by the town's, ever came close to what the swan had been. Something in the particular convergence of the swan's design, the season's unusually fine sand, and Davor's own hand at exactly that point in his skill had produced a piece that simply could not be summoned back on command, however much a wealthy patron was willing to pay for the attempt.

The heron, in particular, cost him something he had not anticipated when he agreed to build it. He had priced the commission generously, on the private assumption that whatever he made would carry something of the swan's magic simply by virtue of coming from the same hands, and when the finished piece proved merely very good rather than extraordinary, the patron who had commissioned it — a shipping merchant who had seen the swan at the Founders' Feast and wanted, in his own words, "something of the same kind for my own hall" — made no secret of his disappointment, and the story of that disappointment traveled the harbor road nearly as quickly as the swan's triumph once had. Davor told me afterward that the heron had taught him something the swan itself never could have: that a reputation built on a single extraordinary piece carries an invisible promise attached to it, a promise that every piece after it will somehow measure up, and that the promise itself, entirely unspoken and never actually made by Davor to anyone, was nonetheless the thing that made the heron's very competence feel, to its buyer, like a small betrayal.

He told me once about a particular commission he nearly refused outright during this period, from a minor noble household two towns south who had heard of the swan secondhand and wanted, in their own words, "something equally magnificent, whatever the cost." Davor spent three sleepless nights weighing whether to take it at all, finally accepting only after negotiating the terms down to something considerably more modest than the household had first proposed — a decorative bowl rather than a sculpture, priced honestly for what a bowl was worth rather than inflated toward what the household seemed willing to pay for a second miracle. "I could have taken their money for a promise I knew I probably couldn't keep," he told me. "I have thought since that this may have been the single wisest decision of my whole career, and almost nobody but the household steward and I ever knew I'd made it, because refusing to overpromise doesn't make for much of a story afterward."

A younger glassblower named Corliss Fen's own son, apprenticed briefly to Davor in those years before finishing his training elsewhere, told me once that the workshop under Davor's post-swan management had developed a quiet, almost superstitious rule among its apprentices: no one was permitted to mention the swan by name during working hours, on the theory, half joking and half entirely sincere, that speaking of it too often invited every subsequent piece to be measured against it before it had even left the furnace. Davor confirmed the rule existed when I asked him about it, though he laughed at how seriously his own apprentices had apparently taken it. "I did not forbid the word out of superstition, exactly," he said. "I forbade it because I noticed my own hands got worse, not better, on the days someone brought it up first thing in the morning. Whatever you want to call that, I decided it was worth protecting against."

This troubled Davor more than the near-ruin had, in a way he found difficult to explain to people who had not lived through it. "Everyone wants me to be the man who made the swan," he told me once, some years afterward, "and I am, in the sense that I did make it. But I cannot make it again, and I have come to think that a reputation built on a single unrepeatable piece is a strange kind of wealth to hold, because it is not actually a description of what I can reliably do. It is a description of one afternoon, a long time ago, that happened to go extraordinarily well."

I want to be fair to the patrons in this story as well, because it would be easy to make them sound fickle in a way I do not think they actually were. Guen Pell herself, when I once had occasion to mention Davor's later struggle to match the swan, seemed genuinely puzzled by the idea that he ought to have been able to. "I did not commission a swan because I believed Davor Quill could produce astonishment on command," she told me. "I commissioned it because I had watched his trial piece and believed he had a real chance at something extraordinary, knowing full well he might fail entirely. He did not fail. That he could not simply repeat it afterward does not surprise me in the least — I have never once expected lightning to strike the same tree by request, and I do not think Davor should have expected it of himself either, though I understand why the rest of the harbor road did."

Isbet Voll, whose own blue had by then been reliably produced across some twenty-five years without a single dramatic collapse or a single dramatic triumph to match the swan's fame, put the contrast to me plainly one afternoon, watching Davor's workshop from across the harbor road. "My name will never be spoken the way his was spoken the season of the swan," she said. "But mine has been spoken, quietly, every season for twenty-five years, by every household in this town that owns a piece of my blue and knows exactly what they'll get if they order another. I would rather be trusted for the twenty-fifth time than astonished once. The twenty-fifth time, a person can actually build a life around. The once, you can only ever stand next to."

I pressed her once, gently, on whether she had ever wanted the kind of attention Davor received, even briefly, even knowing what she now knew about its costs. She considered the question with real seriousness before answering, which told me she had actually thought about it rather than simply reaching for the comfortable answer. "There was a season, my ninth or tenth year, when I could have attempted something larger," she said. "A merchant offered to fund an ambitious commission not unlike Guen Pell's swan, on rather generous terms. I turned it down, not because I doubted I could do it, but because I had already begun to understand, even that early, that the twenty-five quiet years I wanted required a kind of steadiness a single spectacular gamble might interrupt. I have wondered, now and then, what that commission might have become. I have not once regretted the choosing not to find out."

The younger glassblowers of the quarter, in the years following the swan's fame, split fairly evenly, by my own rough count, between those who spoke of Davor as the standard to aspire to and those who spoke, more quietly, of Isbet instead. It was Tamzin, my own granddaughter, still young at the time, who put the distinction to me most plainly, having heard both stories told and retold around the Cinderquay's furnace doors. "Everyone wants to be Davor the year of the swan," she said. "Almost nobody wants to be Davor the two years after it. I think that's the part of his story people leave out when they tell it to impress each other."

I do not think Davor would have disagreed with her, by the later years of his career, though I think it took him longer than it took Isbet to arrive at the same understanding, having tasted, however briefly and however costly, what the once actually felt like. He built, eventually, a steady and well-regarded workshop much like hers — reliable, unglamorous, quietly profitable across decades rather than dramatically celebrated across a single season — and when a young glassblower once asked him, admiringly, how he had learned to make the swan, he gave an answer the young man repeated to me afterward, because it had struck him as stranger than he expected. "I didn't learn to make the swan," Davor said. "I made the swan once, the way lightning happens once in a particular spot. What I learned afterward, the slower and much less exciting way, was how to make an ordinary cup so reliably that a person could order forty of them and receive forty nearly identical to the last."

A single spectacular success and a reputation built on consistency are not simply different sizes of the same wealth. They are different kinds of wealth entirely, and only one of them can be relied upon to still be there the following season. The swan made Davor Quill famous for an afternoon. It was the twenty-five years of reliable blue, made the same careful way every single time, that actually let Isbet Voll build a life on what she'd made.

Guen Pell's swan, incidentally, still stands, so far as I know, in the same hall it was first displayed in, passed down now through two further generations of her family, each of whom has been told, in turn, the story of the year it nearly ruined the man who made it. I like to think that detail belongs somewhere near the end of this particular story, because it is easy, hearing only of Davor's later struggle, to forget that the swan itself was real, and beautiful, and has now outlasted every person who stood in that hall the night it was unveiled — proof, of a kind, that the single spectacular piece and the steady reliable trade are not actually enemies of one another, however much grief the first one caused the man who made it. They are simply two different debts, owed on two entirely different schedules, and a wise craftsman learns, eventually, which one is due first.

I have met, over the years, enough makers who have produced one such piece to recognize a pattern in what comes after. There is almost always a period — months, sometimes longer — in which they cannot work at all, or work only badly, chasing the ghost of what they have already done. The swan casts a long shadow. It becomes a measuring stick against which every subsequent effort is found wanting, and the maker, who ought to know better, begins to believe that the peak has already passed, that everything from here forward will be merely competent, merely good enough, and never again transcendent.

This is, I think, a misunderstanding of what the unrepeatable piece actually represents. It is not the ceiling of one's ability, frozen forever at the height reached on one particular afternoon. It is instead a kind of proof — evidence that the conditions for such work exist, that they can, under the right conjunction of need and skill and circumstance, be met. The swan does not say, *You will never do this again.* It says, *You did this once.* The difference matters.

What the maker learns, if they are patient, is that the unrepeatable piece and the daily work are not stages in a single progression, where one replaces the other. They are parallel tracks. The swan does not obsolete the salad bowls. It simply confirms that both belong to the same hand, and that a life spent making things will, if it is long enough and honest enough, contain room for both the thing that astonishes and the thing that serves.

I do not know if Davor made another swan. I have never asked, and the people who knew him well enough to say are no longer around to tell me. But I know that he kept working, and that the years after that single extraordinary night were filled with chairs and chests and tables that people used and valued, and that when he died, it was not the swan alone that people remembered, but the fact that he had been, all his life, a man who made things worth keeping. That seems to me as much as any of us can reasonably hope to leave behind.

The many shapes glass takes are a testament to human ingenuity, but Marcus found that rebuilding systems had its own rigid forms--and unforgiving consequences.

IX. The Free Hand

Sella Marsh's workshop wasn't filled with masterpieces; it was overflowing with students—a testament to her belief that knowledge shouldn't be hoarded, but shared.

I recall a particular morning when a merchant's son, no more than twelve, wandered into Sella's workshop uninvited, drawn by the sound of her blowpipe, and stood watching in the doorway for the better part of an hour rather than being sent away, as most masters along the harbor road would have sent him. Sella noticed him eventually, and rather than shoo him off, she handed him a scrap of warm glass on the end of a cool rod and let him feel, for himself, how it moved under gentle pressure — an idle kindness, costing her almost nothing, that the boy apparently spoke of for years afterward to anyone who would listen, and that his own household, grateful in a way that outlasted the small gesture itself, remembered when a much larger commission came their way a decade later and they had their pick of any workshop in the quarter to give it to.

Kester Doune, whose own story of chasing Isbet Voll's blue appears earlier in this book, was in most respects Sella's opposite in temperament, though the two of them worked less than a street apart for most of their careers, close enough that their two furnace doors, on certain still mornings, seemed almost to breathe smoke at each other across the narrow lane between them. Kester guarded whatever small techniques he developed with a wariness that bordered on suspicion, refusing even casual questions from apprentices not his own, on the theory — reasonable enough on its face — that any knowledge given away for free was a future competitor strengthened at his own direct expense.

For a number of years, this looked, to anyone watching the Cinderquay from the outside, like the more sensible approach of the two. Kester's techniques, closely held, remained his alone for longer than they might have otherwise, and he built a modestly successful workshop on the strength of that carefulness. Sella, meanwhile, watched no fewer than six young glassblowers she had personally taught go on to open their own workshops nearby, several of them producing work close enough to her own style that a stranger to the quarter might easily have confused one for the other.

I remember one of those six with particular clarity, a boy named Tobin who came to Sella's workshop at fourteen with no family in the trade and no coin to pay for a proper apprenticeship, having been turned away already from two other workshops for exactly that reason. Sella took him on anyway, taught him for four years without ever once asking what he could offer her in return beyond his willingness to learn, and when he opened his own small stall two streets over in his eighteenth year, several of the harbor road's established glassblowers privately predicted he would fail within a season, being both young and unconnected. He did not fail. He came to Sella often in those early years, not for coin or materials but simply for advice, and she gave it as freely as she had given everything else, watching him build, slowly, a small stable trade that in time became one of the more respected young workshops on that stretch of the quarter — a trade that existed, by Tobin's own frequent and unembarrassed admission, only because a woman with no obligation to him had once decided his four years of asking questions were worth answering.

What neither Kester nor the wider quarter fully appreciated, watching this unfold across those same years, was what Sella's open hand was actually building alongside the competition it appeared, on its face, to be creating. Every glassblower she had taught freely carried, afterward, a specific and lasting goodwill toward her that no amount of technical secrecy could have purchased at any price — and when those glassblowers, established now in their own right, found themselves with more custom than they could handle in a busy season, or with a commission better suited to Sella's particular strengths than their own, they sent the buyer to her, without hesitation, the way a person recommends a teacher they have never stopped being grateful to.

Kester, by contrast, found that his careful guardedness bought him exactly what it promised — sole ownership of his own small techniques — and very little else. When his own busy seasons came, no fellow glassblower felt any particular pull to send overflow custom his way, because he had given none of them any reason to think of him as anything other than a careful competitor watching his own interests. When a difficult commission arrived that suited another workshop's particular strength better than his own, he had no network of goodwill to hand it to, and either turned it away or attempted it poorly himself, unwilling to admit that someone two doors down might genuinely serve the buyer better.

There was one particular winter, harder than most, when a fever swept through the Cinderquay and left Kester too ill for nearly six weeks to tend his own furnace at all. Sella's workshop, by contrast, found itself quietly and unexpectedly covered during a similar illness that struck her the following year — three of her former apprentices, Tobin among them, took turns tending her furnace and fulfilling her outstanding orders without being asked, simply because word had reached them that she was unwell, and none of them considered it a debt being repaid so much as an obvious thing a person did for someone who had once done the same for them. Kester's own six weeks passed with no such help arriving, not because his neighbors wished him ill, but because none of them had ever been given any particular reason to think of his trouble as their own concern. He lost, in that stretch, nearly the whole of a season's custom to workshops that simply stayed open while his did not, and told me afterward that it was the empty furnace room during those six weeks, more than any of his failed batches chasing Isbet's blue, that finally made him reconsider the whole shape of how he had built his working life.

Sella's own master, decades before, had been notably the opposite kind of teacher — guarded, withholding, quick to remind an apprentice that knowledge freely given was value freely lost — and Sella told me once that her entire practice of open teaching had begun, in part, as a deliberate rebellion against the particular loneliness of that apprenticeship, a loneliness she had promised herself, watching her own master grow old with few visitors and fewer friends in the trade, that she would not repeat in her own later years. "He was respected," she said of her old master. "Nobody in the quarter would have said an unkind word about his skill. But when he died, three people came to the small gathering afterward, and I was one of them out of a sense of obligation more than affection. I decided, fairly early, that I did not want that particular kind of respected loneliness for myself, whatever it cost me in guarded techniques."

I asked Sella once, watching this pattern play out across a decade or more, whether she ever resented having trained glassblowers who went on to compete directly against her own workshop. She considered the question longer than I expected before answering. "A few of them, in a few bad months, probably did take custom from me that I might otherwise have had," she said. "But I have never once, in all my years, needed to send a difficult commission anywhere and had nowhere to send it, and I have never once had a slow season that a former apprentice, remembering what I once gave them for nothing, did not quietly help me through in some way I hadn't even asked for. I think I have been paid back, many times over, in a currency Kester never learned to accept as real payment, because it never arrived stamped with a fee."

Kester's own late-career turn toward Isbet, asking finally for the knowledge he had spent years trying to steal by imitation instead of simply requesting, taught him something of this lesson from the receiving end, though he told me once that it took him considerably longer to learn to give the same freely to others than it had taken him to finally ask for it himself. "I understand now what it costs to be the kind of workshop nobody feels any warmth toward," he said, in his later years, by then somewhat softened from the guarded young man he had once been. "I am trying to be a different kind of neighbor to the apprentices coming up now than I was to the ones who came up alongside me. It is slower to see the return on than I expected. I am starting to believe that is simply what the return on this particular kind of generosity always looks like."

Sella and Kester, in their final working years, became something closer to genuine friends than either of them would once have predicted, meeting most evenings for a shared pot of tea in the square much as Rasmus Ilde had once done alone, trading small observations about the day's trade with an ease that seemed, to anyone who remembered their younger selves, faintly remarkable. Kester told me once, in one of those final years, that he had come to think of Sella's open hand not as foolishness at all, the way he'd first assumed, but as a considerably harder discipline than his own guardedness had ever required of him. "It costs nothing to keep a secret," he said. "It costs something real, every single time, to give one away for nothing. I spent thirty years thinking the harder path was the one that guarded its knowledge. I have come around, slowly and later than I'd like to admit, to thinking it might have been the other way round the whole time."

Knowledge held tightly protects what it protects, and nothing more. Knowledge given freely builds something a closed hand can never build for itself — a web of goodwill that returns, in its own unpredictable timing, exactly when a workshop most needs an unasked-for kindness. Sella's competitors were real. So was everything they sent back to her, over the years, that Kester's careful solitude never once received from anyone.

Emrys' unbroken run was remarkable, and Petran's miscalculation proved an important lesson about the tide merchant's patience—but what happens when even *that* patience runs out?

X. The Many Shapes

The chipped ceramic mug warmed Eleanor's hands, though the tea inside had long since gone cold. She watched Old Man Tiber carefully arranging a display of sea-worn stones outside his curio shop.

Eleanor found herself thinking about Ysolt Kane and Marl Ashen as she watched him. Two workshops, two apprenticeships forged in the same heat, yet diverging paths that always seemed to circle back to this quiet question: how much of yourself do you spread across the world, and how much do you hold tightly within your own hands? She'd spent years documenting their parallel careers, charting the slow drift between Ysolt's expanding repertoire and Marl's stubborn focus. It wasn't about talent—both were gifted glassblowers—but something deeper. Something most founders missed entirely until it was too late.

She remembered a conversation with Silas Blackwood, the shipyard owner. A man who built ships but rarely sailed them. "Everyone thinks diversification is safety," he'd rasped over a shared lunch of salt cod and hardtack. "They believe spreading your risk means diminishing your exposure. That's only true if you assume all risks are equal." He'd paused, spearing a piece of fish with his fork. "But some risks *are* the point. Some bets are worth doubling down on."

That had felt abstract then, even dismissive. A wealthy man's pronouncement about risk from a position of comfortable distance. Now, watching Tiber coax stability out of chaos, Eleanor realized Blackwood hadn't been talking about wealth at all. He'd been talking about focus. About the cost of dilution.

Ysolt, in those early years, had operated under a simple logic: more skills meant more customers. A wider range of offerings seemed like insurance against fickle tastes or seasonal downturns. If the demand for ornate goblets waned, she could pivot to practical windowpanes. No single patron held her livelihood hostage. It felt…sensible. Safe.

But what Eleanor had begun to see, digging through ledgers and interviewing former customers, was that 'safe' wasn't necessarily sustainable. Ysolt hadn't built a foundation; she'd assembled a collection of shifting sands. Every new skill acquired meant another area where she was merely *competent*, not exceptional. She spread herself so thin that no single craft had the chance to truly deepen, to become something genuinely remarkable.

You might be thinking this sounds like a simple case of specialization versus generalization, the familiar refrain of every business consultant since time began. But it wasn't about avoiding breadth entirely. Eleanor hadn't seen Ysolt's workshop or Marl's during their early years—she hadn't been born yet when they first set up shop—but she had talked to those who had. She understood the initial appeal of versatility. The problem wasn't that Ysolt *could* make many things; it was that she became defined by her ability to do so, rather than by what she did best.

Marl, on the other hand, had made a different gamble. He'd chosen floats—simple, unglamorous fishing floats—and refused to deviate. Most established glassblowers considered it beneath them, a monotonous task suitable only for apprentices. They envisioned elegant decanters and intricate sculptures; Marl focused on a humble sphere that bobbed in the waves.

Eleanor remembered one particularly vivid account from Old Man Hemlock, a retired fisherman who'd known Marl since boyhood. "Everyone laughed at him," Hemlock had said, his voice raspy with age. "Said he was wasting his talent on something a child could learn to blow. But then the storms came. And every crew that relied on Marl's floats—they kept fishing. Nets stayed afloat when others were lost."

It wasn't just about quality, though the floats *were* exceptionally well-made. It was about reputation. About becoming synonymous with a single, vital need. When a captain needed new floats, he didn't ask for quotes from multiple workshops; he went straight to Marl Ashen. Because Marl hadn't just mastered a technique—he had become the keeper of a critical lifeline.

And that, Eleanor suspected, was where most businesses faltered. They mistook activity for progress. They chased every opportunity, said 'yes' to every request, believing that volume would eventually translate into value. But in a crowded marketplace, it wasn't about doing more; it was about becoming indispensable at *one* thing.

She thought of her own second year consulting. Landing the Fortune 500 client—Harrow & Finch—had felt like a breakthrough. Nine months spent crafting a bespoke strategic framework, complete with color-coded binders, custom metrics, and enough PowerPoint slides to wallpaper a cathedral. They'd lauded it, praised its meticulous detail, implemented every recommendation. And then she'd tried to apply the same system to her next three clients—a small brewery, a textile mill, and a shipping concern. It hadn't worked. Not even close.

She had built a monument to Harrow & Finch's specific quirks instead of isolating the underlying principles that actually drove success. She'd been so focused on *appearing* comprehensive that she'd failed to create anything genuinely transferable. The realization stung, even now.

It wasn't about being brilliant at everything; it was about being ruthlessly selective about what truly mattered. What core competency could you nurture until it bloomed into something extraordinary? What problem could you solve so completely that customers would seek *you* out specifically, regardless of price?

Eleanor glanced back at Old Man Tiber, who had finally stepped back from his arrangement, surveying his work with a critical eye. A gentle breeze shifted the stones slightly, threatening to unravel the precarious balance. He didn't rush to fix it; he simply adjusted one pebble, then another, reinforcing the connections, subtly shifting the weight until the whole structure settled into a new equilibrium.

He wasn't trying to build an impenetrable fortress. He was creating something resilient—something that could withstand the inevitable forces of change by adapting and rebalancing. It wasn't about eliminating risk; it was about distributing it intelligently. About knowing which elements were essential, and which could be sacrificed without compromising the whole.

Ysolt's initial advantage—her versatility—had become her undoing. As other workshops adopted her broad approach, competition intensified, driving down prices and eroding her margins. She found herself trapped in a race to the bottom, offering adequate products at increasingly unsustainable rates. Marl, meanwhile, had carved out a niche so deep that he was virtually untouchable. Demand for his floats remained constant, even as Ysolt struggled to stay afloat.

Eleanor wondered what might have happened if Ysolt had recognized her strength earlier—if she'd identified the one craft within her repertoire that truly ignited her passion and focused all her energy on mastering it. She eventually did narrow her focus to decorative mirrors, but by then, years of scattered effort had left her playing catch-up. The damage was done.

The cost of inaction isn't always a sudden catastrophe; it's often a slow erosion of potential. A gradual dilution of strength until what once shone brightly fades into mediocrity. And the saddest part? It rarely feels like a conscious choice. Most founders don't deliberately set out to spread themselves thin. They simply mistake motion for progress, activity for value.

Eleanor finished her cold tea and set the mug aside. The sun was beginning to dip towards the horizon, casting long shadows across the Cinderquay. Tiber had moved on to sweeping the sidewalk in front of his shop, meticulously clearing away any debris that might deter a potential customer.

What if, instead of asking *what else* you can do, you asked *what will you refuse*? What opportunities must you deliberately turn down—not because they're undesirable, but because they distract you from your true north? The question hung in the air, heavy and unresolved. And Eleanor knew, with a certainty that settled deep within her bones, that it was a question every founder needed to answer before their kiln went cold.

Tiber had moved on to sweeping the sidewalk in front of his shop, meticulously clearing away any debris that might deter a potential customer. The rhythm of the broom against the worn stone was almost hypnotic, each sweep a small act of defiance against the inevitable accumulation of dust and ash that plagued the Cinderquay. Eleanor watched him for a moment, considering the simple dedication in the movement, the quiet insistence on maintaining order in a world perpetually tilting towards entropy. It wasn't about cleanliness, not exactly. It was about declaring *this space*, this small patch of ground before his workshop, as something worth caring for.

What if, instead of asking *what else* you can do, you asked *what will you refuse*? What opportunities must you deliberately turn down—not because they're undesirable, but because they distract you from your true north? The question hung in the air, heavy and unresolved. And Eleanor knew, with a certainty that settled deep within her bones, that it was a question every founder needed to answer before their kiln went cold.

I remember my second year consulting, landing a Fortune 500 client and spending nine months building a bespoke strategic framework just for them—color-coded binders, custom metrics, the works. They loved it. I genuinely believed I'd cracked some universal code of organizational efficiency. Then I tried to take what I'd learned to my next three clients and discovered none of it transferred. None of it. I'd built a monument to one company's quirks instead of isolating what actually mattered, mistaking specificity for insight. The binders gathered dust on my shelf, a silent indictment of my own hubris. It was an expensive lesson in the difference between tailoring a solution and building a cage.

Ysolt had believed she was spreading her risk, diversifying against the whims of the market. Marl, by contrast, hadn't been thinking about markets at all. He'd been thinking about his father, about nets lost to shoddy equipment, about something *reliable* in a sea of uncertainty. And that difference—that seemingly small divergence in motivation—had grown into a chasm over time. It wasn't about being clever or strategic. It was about what you cared enough about to defend, relentlessly, against the constant pressure to do just…more.

Eleanor pictured Ysolt's workshop, crammed with half-finished projects, each competing for attention, each demanding a sliver of her limited focus. She imagined the quiet order of Marl's shop, the stacks of perfectly formed floats, identical yet somehow unique in their subtle variations, like a field of green glass stretching towards the horizon. One was a kaleidoscope, the other a lens. Both could capture light, but only one offered true clarity.

The cost wasn't just economic—though Ysolt's dwindling profits were certainly a symptom. It was something deeper, a slow erosion of competence, a dilution of expertise. Each new skill she added wasn't an addition to her capabilities; it was a subtraction from the others. She hadn't become more capable overall; she'd become adequately passable at many things, and truly excellent at none. And in a market that increasingly rewarded excellence—or even just consistent reliability—adequacy simply wasn't enough.

Think of a sculptor working with clay. They can try to sculpt ten different figures simultaneously, spreading their attention across multiple forms. The result will likely be ten unfinished, mediocre pieces. Or they can focus all their energy on a single figure, refining every curve, perfecting every detail, until it comes alive under their hands. Which sculpture is more likely to endure? Which one will people remember?

It wasn't about avoiding variety altogether. Variety had its place, particularly in the initial stages of exploration. It was about recognizing when exploration needed to give way to focus, when breadth needed to be traded for depth. The danger wasn't in trying new things; it was in *staying* with too many new things, never allowing any one of them to truly take root.

Eleanor remembered a conversation she'd had with Old Man Hemlock, the shipwright down at the docks, years ago. He'd been building boats his entire life, and he'd once told her that the secret to a strong vessel wasn't just in the quality of the materials, but in the number of unnecessary features you left out. "Every extra beam," Hemlock had said, his voice raspy with salt air, "is another point of failure. Every ornament is another place for rot to set in." He'd built boats that weren't beautiful, not exactly. They were *reliable*. And in the unforgiving waters of Ashmere, reliability was a form of beauty all its own.

You might be thinking this sounds restrictive—that it demands a kind of ruthless pruning of possibilities. That it smothers creativity. And you wouldn't be entirely wrong to think that. It *is* restrictive. It *does* demand difficult choices. But what's the alternative? A life spent chasing every fleeting opportunity, scattering your energy until nothing remains? A workshop filled with half-finished projects and unrealized potential?

The truth is, saying "no" isn't about limiting yourself; it's about liberating yourself. It's about reclaiming control over your time, your energy, your attention. It's about creating the space you need to do truly meaningful work. Every "yes" requires a corresponding "no." The question isn't whether you *can* do something; it's whether you can afford not to do everything else.

Eleanor glanced back at Tiber, who was now meticulously arranging a display of small glass birds in his window—each one delicate and exquisitely crafted. He hadn't built a wide-ranging workshop. He didn't offer goblets or mirrors or strung beads. He made birds. Just birds. And people traveled from across the quarter to buy them, not because they were the cheapest, but because they were undeniably *good*. Because Tiber had spent years honing his craft, mastering every nuance of glass and feather, until he could create something truly special.

The sun dipped lower, painting the Cinderquay in shades of orange and gold. The air grew cooler, carrying the scent of salt and woodsmoke. Eleanor wrapped her shawl tighter around her shoulders and turned to leave. She wasn't sure what Ysolt was working on now—whether she'd found a new niche or simply resigned herself to a quiet existence. But she knew one thing for certain: the lesson of the glassblowers extended far beyond the workshop walls. It was a lesson about focus, about discipline, about the courage to say "no" to everything that didn't align with your true north.

And as she walked away from the Long Kiln, Eleanor found herself wondering what *she* was willing to refuse. What glittering distractions had she been chasing at the expense of something more meaningful? What opportunities had she embraced simply because they felt urgent, rather than important? The questions weren't easy—and she didn't expect them to be. But she knew that answering them honestly was the first step towards building a foundation strong enough to withstand the inevitable storms.

What single thing, if you lost it tomorrow, would leave the largest hole in your life? Not the most convenient, not the most lucrative, but the one thing you could not replace without fundamentally altering who you are. Don't start looking for that thing. Start asking yourself what you're willing to let go of *today* to create space for it. Because the shape of your future isn't determined by the things you add—it's defined by the things you subtract.

Each stone seemed to lean against the next, supporting and supported, forming a precarious balance that defied any breeze.

Corra Fenn sought to preserve a memory in glass, but Joset Corvane had other plans that made her ask if she was seeing things clearly.

XI. The Second Furnace

I still remember the exact moment I knew Marcus was going to lose his company—it wasn't a single catastrophic event, but an accumulation of small fixes masking a fundamental flaw.

"This one's elegant," he said, scrolling through code I couldn't read. "Way cheaper than the nuclear option."

The nuclear option was his term for rebuilding the foundation. He'd gotten quotes: six weeks of development, zero new features shipped, maybe some angry customers during the transition. The patch cost $18,000. The rebuild would've been $90,000.

Marcus had raised three rounds of funding by then. Smart money, good investors, everyone bullish on the SaaS model. And he was burning it all on patches.

"The thing is," I said, watching him scroll, "you're going to pay for the rebuild eventually. Question is whether you pay for it on your schedule or the system's."

He laughed. Actual laughter. "Can't afford to stop revenue for six weeks. Not with the board breathing down my neck about growth."

The system collapsed on Black Friday—his biggest sales day of the year. The database couldn't handle the load. Transactions failed. Customers got charged multiple times or not at all. The patches had been introducing tiny inconsistencies for months, and under real pressure the whole structure just folded.

He was out of business by January.

I think about Marcus every time I hear someone say they can't afford to stop and fix the foundation. Because what they mean is: *I can't afford the* appearance *of stopping.* But there's a second kind of stopping that's worse, and you don't get to choose when it happens.

Ivo Meer's second furnace wasn't a billing system, but the pattern was identical.

Ivo had run his workshop for fifteen years before the commission arrived. Fifteen years of careful expansion—a second workbench in year four, a larger annealing oven in year nine, an apprentice (Guen Farrow) in year twelve. Each addition came *after* he'd earned the money to pay for it. His father had been a fisherman on the North Sea, and the advice was fisherman's wisdom: never rig more sail than your boat can carry, no matter how promising the wind looks.

The commission came from a merchant fleet replacing their entire run of ships. They needed lanterns. Hundreds of them. Ivo's single furnace could maybe produce a third of the order by their deadline.

He could've declined the portion he couldn't handle. Or he could borrow money, build a second furnace, and take the whole commission.

The second path wasn't reckless. The fleet had been in business for forty years. They'd told him this was the first run of ships in a planned expansion—more orders would follow. And the math worked: if even half the promised future orders materialized, the second furnace would pay for itself in three years.

Ivo borrowed the money and built the furnace.

The first commission went perfectly. The fleet was delighted. They hinted strongly at the next order, talked about timelines, mentioned they were opening two new trade routes.

Then the waiting started.

A difficult season at sea pushed their next ship launch back six months. Then the fleet changed ownership—a buyout by a larger concern—and the new owners wanted to "review all supplier relationships." The next order didn't come in six months. It didn't come in a year.

Ivo now had two furnaces, twice the fuel costs, wages for an additional apprentice, and debt payments every month regardless of how much work came through the door.

He had other clients, sized to a one-furnace operation. The kind of orders that kept one furnace busy left the second furnace cold most days. Running a furnace at partial capacity is expensive—you still burn fuel to keep it hot enough to work, but you're only producing at sixty percent.

So Ivo started borrowing again. Not to expand. To cover operating costs while he waited for the promised orders to materialize.

He spent two years in that trap. Two years of watching his debt grow while the second furnace sat mostly idle. He stopped coming to the Long Kiln as often—the communal kiln where glassblowers gathered to talk shop. When he did come, he talked less about his work and more about shipping routes, trade winds, fleet management decisions. Things outside his control that nevertheless controlled his future.

Guen Farrow, his eldest apprentice, basically ran the workshop during those two years. She'd been with him for eight years by then, skilled enough to handle most orders without supervision. Ivo told me later he wasn't sure the workshop would've survived without her.

I met Ivo during the second year of the lean period. He came to the Long Kiln one evening, watched the coals for a while, then asked me a question that clearly wasn't casual: "You ever seen a workshop fall apart from what seemed like a reasonable mistake?"

"More often than from an unreasonable one," I said. "Unreasonable mistakes are obvious. You see them coming. Reasonable ones hide until it's too late."

The fleet did eventually resume orders. New ownership settled, the trade routes proved profitable, and Ivo became their primary supplier for lanterns. The second furnace became a sound investment over the next decade.

But those two years marked him. He'd learned a distinction he wished he'd understood earlier: you can grow by earning first and spending after, or you can grow by borrowing first and earning later. For fifteen years he'd done the former without thinking about it.

The latter put him at the mercy of timelines he didn't control.

"Should've just declined the commission," I said when he told me the full story.

He shook his head. "Mistake wasn't taking the commission. Mistake was thinking one large order meant I needed permanent capacity for large orders. I could've phased it. Built the second furnace after I had three commissions that size, not one."

The opportunity tends to be large and immediate—*this* commission, *this* partnership, *this* market window. The cost reveals itself slowly, in a thousand small ways you didn't forecast.

Ivo gave Guen a partnership stake the year after he stabilized. She'd earned it. More than that, her steadiness during the crisis had taught him something: when he was under pressure, he got worse at running the workshop. She got better.

The second furnace ran profitably for years. The fleet became his most reliable client, exactly as promised. By every external measure, the gamble paid off.

But Ivo never called it a success. "A gamble that pays off is still a gamble," he said. "I measure it by what I understood when I made the choice, not by how it turned out."

Marcus and Ivo made the exact same category of mistake, but it looked completely different in each case.

Marcus kept patching because stopping to rebuild felt too expensive. Ivo built the second furnace because *not* expanding felt too expensive. One was trying to avoid a cost, the other was trying to capture an opportunity. Both misjudged the cost of being wrong.

The pattern underneath is identical: they were steering by what felt affordable *in the moment*, not by what they could actually afford if conditions shifted.

Marcus couldn't afford six weeks of halted revenue—or so he thought. What he actually couldn't afford was the seventh patch, which bought him another four months before the system collapsed permanently. But he didn't know that at the time.

Ivo couldn't afford to turn down the commission—or so he thought. What he actually couldn't afford was two years of debt payments on a furnace he couldn't keep busy. But the future orders seemed certain, right up until they didn't.

The question I keep circling back to: how do you know which kind of stopping you're choosing? The kind that positions you for the future, or the kind that just delays a reckoning?

I've asked that question to maybe fifty business owners over the years. The honest ones admit they're guessing. The overconfident ones tell me they've "run the numbers." But numbers only tell you what happens if your assumptions are right.

What Ivo eventually learned—what Marcus never got the chance to learn—is that the real question isn't whether to invest in growth. It's whether you're building capacity for demand that's already proven, or capacity for demand you're hoping will materialize.

One is expansion. The other is speculation.

They look similar in the moment. The difference only becomes obvious later, when you're either running both furnaces at capacity or paying debt on equipment you can't keep busy.

The year after Ivo gave Guen her partnership stake, they took on another large commission—a different fleet, similar size to the first. Ivo told me he and Guen spent two weeks debating whether they could handle it with existing capacity or needed to expand again.

"What decided it?" I asked.

"I asked her: if this commission disappears tomorrow, are we better off with three furnaces than two? She thought about it for maybe ten seconds and said no."

They declined half the order. Took what they could handle with existing capacity. The fleet found another supplier for the rest.

"Did you lose the relationship?"

"No. They appreciated the honesty. And when the second order came—which it did, six months later—they gave us the whole thing because we'd delivered the first half flawlessly."

That's the version of the story Ivo wishes he'd lived the first time. Not avoiding growth. Not refusing opportunity. Just refusing to build permanent capacity for temporary certainty.

Most of the founders I work with aren't failing because they're too conservative. They're failing because they can't tell the difference between an investment that positions them for proven demand and an investment that requires the future to cooperate.

You're going to face a version of this choice. Maybe you already have. Someone's going to offer you something that requires you to expand *now* based on what seems likely to happen *later*. The opportunity will be real. The risk will be hidden in assumptions you don't realize you're making.

Before you build that second furnace—whatever form it takes in your business—ask yourself Guen's question: if the future order disappears tomorrow, are you better off having expanded or not?

If the answer is anything other than a clear yes, you're not looking at an investment. You're looking at a bet.

And the house you're betting is the one you've spent years building.

Rurik's misfortune highlighted the common purse of all artisans—and Maren Holt's gamble revealed the true cost of cheap materials.

XII. The Unbroken Run

I watched Emrys Thale carry his first set of impossibly thin lamp globes into the Long Kiln on a cold morning in November, and what struck me most was not their fragility, but the quiet confidence with which he carried them.

"I kept waiting for it to go wrong," he told me. "It never did."

He said it like a confession.

"I don't entirely know what I did differently, and that troubles me more than it probably should."

I told him not knowing why a piece succeeded was no great sin, so long as he didn't mistake the not-knowing for a secret he'd already solved. I don't think he heard the second half of what I said. People rarely do, when they're standing in the middle of their first real win.

Here's what I want to name plainly, before I tell you the rest of Emrys's story: success, taken in an unbroken run, teaches a craftsman almost nothing true about himself. It teaches him a great deal that is false.

And the trouble—the particular trouble that wrecked Emrys's workshop and has wrecked more businesses along the harbor road than any shortage of talent or market opportunity ever did—is that the false lessons feel, from the inside, exactly like wisdom.

Emrys kept a modest workshop at the inland edge of the Cinderquay, a street back from the harbor road where the finer frontages stood. For the better part of a decade he'd been entirely ordinary. Competent. Reliable. Capable of good work when good work was asked of him. Not a name anyone in the quarter would have singled out as destined for anything larger than steady, unremarkable trade.

I annealed his pieces for years without any particular story attaching itself to his name. In this trade, that's its own kind of quiet compliment.

The run began—as these things often do—without any sense at the time that it was beginning at all.

A shipping factor along the harbor road wanted a set of unusually thin-walled lamp globes for a new run of vessel lanterns. Thinner than Emrys had ever attempted. Thin enough that a single uneven breath at the pipe could split the whole piece before it left the furnace. Two other workshops with steadier reputations for fine work had already turned the commission down as too great a risk for too modest a fee.

Emrys took it. More out of need than confidence.

To his own evident surprise as much as anyone else's, he produced the full set without a single failure. Globes so thin and so even that the factor ordered twice the original number before the season was out.

That morning in the Long Kiln doorway, watching him turn that globe in the lamplight—I felt something I couldn't name at the time. Not simple admiration. Something closer to unease. The particular unease of a man who has spent forty years at a fire watching what usually follows a run like that one.

I couldn't have told you exactly what I expected to follow it. Only that something in my own long experience of the Long Kiln did not trust an unbroken string of difficulty this clean.

A second commission followed within the same season. A set of nested drinking bowls, so delicately graduated in size that the glazier who ordinarily handled such work had quietly warned the buyer it would likely take two attempts to get right.

Emrys produced the full nested set on his first attempt. Each bowl fitting its neighbor with a precision that made even Isbet Voll—hearing of it secondhand—remark to me that she had not managed anything quite that clean on her own first try at a similarly graduated set, years before.

A third commission came that same winter. Riskier still. A pair of matched vases in a mineral mixture Emrys had never worked with before, prone by reputation to clouding if the furnace ran even slightly too hot.

These, too, came out of his kiln clear and matched and whole.

Three difficult pieces. Each one genuinely harder than the last. Each one completed without a single failure along the way.

Do you see what was happening yet? I didn't, not clearly, though I felt it. Emrys certainly didn't see it. He was too busy learning the wrong lesson.

Here's the thing about caution in any trade: it's a habit built for the moment when everything feels safest.

Emrys had always—before this season—brought me a small trial piece ahead of any large or unfamiliar commission. A scrap-glass test of a new mineral mixture, fired and cooled on its own before he risked committing an entire commission's worth of material to an untested batch. Such an ordinary habit among careful glassblowers in the quarter that I had never once thought to remark on it, in his workshop or anyone else's.

Until the winter he quietly stopped doing it.

He told me, much later, exactly when the habit fell away. It was smaller and less dramatic a moment than I expected.

A merchant's household, hearing of his recent run, came to him with a commission for a full dinner service in a deep garnet red. A color notoriously unstable in the furnace, prone to streaking if the mineral batch was even slightly uneven.

Emrys had, as always, a fresh batch of the mineral on hand. Untested against his own furnace's particular heat.

He stood over it that morning, scrap glass and testing rod within easy reach.

And simply did not use them.

"I remember thinking the test would only tell me what I already knew," he said, later. "Three commissions in a row had gone right without a single surprise. I told myself I had gotten past needing to check, the way a man who has crossed a familiar bridge a hundred times stops looking down at the boards under his feet."

The dinner service came out of his furnace whole. The garnet even and unstreaked across every piece.

You see the trouble, don't you? A habit abandoned and rewarded anyway teaches a craftsman precisely the wrong lesson twice in a row.

Emrys did not test a mineral batch again that entire season.

He told buyers, when they asked how he managed pieces other workshops considered too risky to attempt, that he had simply developed an instinct for the furnace that most glassblowers never fully acquired. I don't think he was lying to them, exactly. I think he had genuinely come to believe it. The way a man standing in unusually calm weather for four crossings running comes to believe he has learned something true about the sea, rather than simply having been fortunate in his timing.

It was Rasmus Ilde—watching this unfold from his usual seat in the square with the particular clarity of a man who had spent his own working decades on boats rather than at furnaces—who said to me privately, well before the trouble finally arrived, that he did not trust what he was seeing.

"I sailed with a captain once who went eleven crossings without losing so much as a barrel to weather," Rasmus told me. "By the ninth crossing he had stopped consulting the glass before he set sail, because eight clean crossings in a row had convinced him he could read a coming storm in his own bones better than any instrument could tell him."

Rasmus paused, the way he always did when he was arriving at the part of a story that mattered.

"The sea did not care how many crossings he'd had. It only cared what was actually coming the twelfth time. And he was not looking at the glass when it came."

He said he saw the same captain in Emrys every time the young man's name came up along the harbor road that winter. Though he admitted he had no way of knowing, any more than anyone else did, which particular commission would be the twelfth crossing.

You might be thinking: surely Emrys had earned the right to trust his instinct by then. Three difficult commissions, each one harder than the last, each one successful. Isn't that exactly what mastery looks like—the ability to feel your way through complexity that would require lesser craftsmen to measure and test and second-guess themselves into paralysis?

Here's what I wish I had said to Emrys that morning in the Long Kiln doorway, plainly enough that he couldn't have failed to hear it:

Success and good judgment can arrive from entirely different directions and look, from the inside, exactly alike.

The three commissions had gone right. That much was true. But they had not gone right *because* Emrys's instinct had suddenly become infallible. They had gone right because his instinct was still being quietly checked—corrected, hedged, confirmed—by the testing and caution he had not yet thought to abandon. The trial pieces. The full cooling times. The margin he built into every furnace load, the same margins that had kept his work ordinary and unremarkable for a decade.

Those habits hadn't stopped mattering. They had only stopped being visible to him, the way the bridge boards under a man's feet stop being visible once he's convinced himself he knows the crossing by heart.

And the moment he stopped testing—the moment he decided his instinct alone was enough—was the exact season those habits would have caught what his instinct could not see.

The fourth ambitious commission arrived that spring.

By any honest measure, it was the largest Emrys had yet attempted: a full matched set of serving glass for a merchant guild's annual feast. Commissioned in a pale rose mineral mixture Emrys had used successfully once before—in the second of his three earlier successes—though in a considerably smaller quantity and a different furnace load than the guild now required.

He did not test the new, larger batch of mineral against a trial piece before committing the whole commission to it. He told himself he had already proven the color once and saw no reason a larger batch of the same general mixture would behave any differently.

He did not, either, allow the full cooling time the piece's unusual thickness would ordinarily have called for. The guild's feast date was fixed, and he had by then come to trust his own judgment about which pieces could safely be hurried more than he trusted the Long Kiln's own patient schedule.

The same schedule, I might add, that this book opened by insisting no glassblower's confidence, however earned, was ever entitled to shorten.

The pieces came out of the annealing looking, to every eye in his workshop, entirely finished.

It was only at the guild feast itself—three weeks later—that the first goblet cracked in a steward's hand while being set on the table. Followed within the same evening by two more. The mineral batch's slight impurity finally showing itself as a network of hairline weaknesses that no amount of confident instinct had ever actually tested for.

The guild's master, humiliated in front of his own membership, sent the remaining pieces back within the week. Word of the failure traveled the harbor road with considerably more speed than word of the three quiet successes that had preceded it.

A single dramatic collapse always outpaces a season of ordinary competence in the retelling.

Emrys came to the Long Kiln the following morning looking, for the first time since the run began, like the same uncertain young man who had stood in my doorway turning that first thin-walled globe in the lamplight.

He did not, at first, understand what had actually gone wrong.

He had convinced himself so thoroughly that his instinct alone had carried the first three commissions that he genuinely could not see—without my help—that instinct had never been the whole of it. That a trial piece tested and a full cooling time honored had been quietly doing real work underneath each of those three successes. Work he had simply stopped noticing because it had never once failed to be there.

"I thought I had learned something about the mineral," he said.

His voice was flat. Defeated.

"I had only been lucky about the mineral, three times, while doing the one thing that would have caught the luck running out. And then I stopped doing it the exact season it would have mattered most."

I let him sit with that for a moment.

Then I told him what I had wanted to tell him the morning he first stood in my doorway with the thin-walled globes, and had not found the right words for at the time.

A run of success—however earned—tells a craftsman nothing about whether his judgment has actually improved. Because success and good judgment can arrive from entirely different directions and look, from the inside, exactly alike.

The only real test of whether a man's instinct has grown past the need for testing is the one commission where the instinct is wrong and the testing would have caught it.

And a man who has stopped testing, by the time that commission arrives, has no way left of finding out until the piece is already in a stranger's hands.

Let me be more specific about what this cost Emrys, because I don't want you to hear this as a story about glassblowing and miss what it's actually about.

The guild did not just send the pieces back. They told the story. And the story they told—the story that mattered along the harbor road—was not that Emrys Thale had successfully completed three ambitious commissions in a row. It was that Emrys Thale had taken a high-profile guild commission, cut corners, and delivered cracked glass to a feast.

It didn't matter that he hadn't actually cut corners in any dishonest sense. He had simply trusted his instinct at the exact moment his instinct stopped being trustworthy. But reputation doesn't care about distinctions that fine.

Three other commissions that had been quietly making their way toward his workshop that spring—commissions from buyers who had heard of the earlier successes and wanted similarly ambitious work—went to other workshops instead. One of them, I happen to know, went to a glassblower who was genuinely less skilled than Emrys but who had the good fortune of not having failed publicly in the same season.

Emrys's workshop, which had been profitable for the first time in years during the winter of the streak, went back to taking the small, safe commissions that paid just enough to cover the furnace and the rent. He told me later that he had been two commissions away from hiring a second glassblower—the first expansion of his workshop in a decade—and that the hire, if it had happened, would have let him take on the kind of larger, steadier trade that might have actually stabilized his business.

Instead, he spent the next eighteen months rebuilding his reputation from the same modest baseline he'd occupied before the run began.

The streak had taught him nothing. The collapse taught him everything.

And the gap between those two moments—the gap between the last successful commission and the first failed one—cost him not just the immediate loss of the guild's payment, but the entire trajectory he'd been building toward during the winter he thought he'd finally figured out how to trust himself.

I want to be honest with you about something, because I think it matters to what comes next in this book, and because I've watched this same pattern repeat itself enough times in enough workshops along the Cinderquay that I no longer believe it's a story about glassblowing at all.

Most businesses don't fail because the founder lacked talent. They don't fail because the market wasn't there. They fail because the founder couldn't tell the difference between a necessary long-term safeguard and an expensive distraction, and by the time they learned the difference, they were out of runway.

Emrys didn't lose the guild commission because he was bad at glassblowing. He lost it because an unbroken run of success had quietly convinced him that the safeguards he'd built into his process—the trial pieces, the full cooling times, the margins—were no longer necessary. That they were, in fact, evidence he hadn't yet learned to trust his own instinct.

And the moment he abandoned those safeguards was the exact moment they would have saved him.

You see this in every trade. The startup founder who raises a successful seed round, then a Series A, then a Series B, and somewhere in the middle of the run stops doing the careful financial modeling that kept the early rounds honest—because three successful raises in a row feel like proof that investors trust his vision, and careful modeling starts to feel like a lack of confidence in that vision. The coach who wins three games in a row with an aggressive play style and stops drilling the fundamentals that made the aggressive style work in the first place—because winning feels like proof the fundamentals were always overrated. The writer who publishes three well-received books and stops revising as carefully, because three books that didn't need heavy revision feel like proof that the first draft is now good enough.

The pattern is always the same. Success, taken in an unbroken run, teaches you that the caution you practiced on the way up was training wheels you've now outgrown. And the moment you stop practicing that caution is the moment you find out whether it was actually training wheels—or load-bearing structure you'd simply stopped noticing.

Emrys rebuilt his reputation slowly across the following several years. The way most of the people in this book eventually rebuilt what a single hard season had cost them.

He returned, from that spring onward, to testing every unfamiliar batch against scrap glass before he risked a commission on it. Whether or not the run behind him made the testing feel, in the moment, like an insult to his own hard-won skill.

He told me once—well into his own later years, long after the failed guild commission had stopped being the first story people told about his workshop—that he had come to think of the three early successes not as proof of anything he'd actually learned, but as a kind of debt quietly accruing interest.

"Three commissions where the caution I'd abandoned had simply not yet been asked to matter," he said. "I used to think the streak was teaching me who I'd become. It wasn't teaching me anything. It was only failing to correct me, three times running, and I mistook the silence for a lesson."

I think about that line often. More often, probably, than any other single thing anyone along the Cinderquay has ever said to me.

Because the silence—the unbroken run where nothing goes wrong, where every risk pays off, where every shortcut you take turns out fine—is not neutral. It is not a lesson. It is only the temporary absence of correction.

And the cost of mistaking that silence for wisdom is always the same: you stop doing the thing that would have caught the trouble, exactly one commission before the commission that needed it.

So what do you do with a run like that, when you're in the middle of it?

How do you hold onto the caution that kept you safe on the way up, when every success makes that caution feel less like wisdom and more like a failure to trust what you've learned?

I don't have a clean answer to that. I wish I did. But here's what I've seen work, in the workshops that survived their own streaks and the workshops that didn't:

The glassblowers who made it through—who kept their caution even when the run made it feel unnecessary—were the ones who had someone in their corner who remembered what the work looked like before the streak began. Someone who could say, plainly and without hedging, *You're not testing the mineral anymore, and that troubles me.* Someone whose job was not to celebrate the wins but to ask the un-celebrated question: *What are you not doing now that you were doing six months ago, and what happens if you need it again?*

Emrys didn't have that person. Or maybe he did—maybe I was supposed to be that person, standing in the Long Kiln doorway the morning he brought in those first thin globes—and I failed to say the thing plainly enough that he couldn't ignore it.

I've thought about that morning more times than I can count. What I could have said differently. Whether it would have mattered.

I still don't know.

But I know this: the next time someone stands in my doorway turning a difficult piece in the lamplight and tells me they don't know why it went right, I'm going to say the second half of what I said to Emrys more plainly than I said it the first time.

Not knowing why a piece succeeded is no sin. But mistaking the not-knowing for a secret you've already solved will cost you the next piece, and the piece after that, and eventually the whole season you thought the streak was building toward.

The run is not the lesson. The run is only the run.

And what you do with the caution you practiced on the way up—whether you keep it or abandon it, whether you treat it as training wheels or as load-bearing structure—is the only question that actually determines whether the streak becomes a foundation or just a brief, expensive detour on the way back to where you started.

There's a commission sitting on my annealing schedule right now that's going to test this in a way I haven't been tested in years. I'm not going to tell you what it is yet—that's a story for later in this book, and I don't know how it ends.

But I will tell you this: I've been doing this work long enough that I could, if I wanted to, skip the trial piece and trust my own instinct about how the mineral will behave in the furnace.

Three decades at the Long Kiln. More successful commissions than I can count. An unbroken run, if I'm being honest, that's lasted longer than Emrys's ever did.

And I'm still going to fire the trial piece first.

Not because I don't trust my instinct. But because I've seen what happens when a man mistakes an unbroken run for proof that his instinct has grown past the need for testing.

The lesson isn't whether to trust yourself. The lesson is knowing that the moment you feel most entitled to trust yourself—the moment the testing feels most like an insult to everything you've learned—is exactly the moment the testing matters most.

Emrys learned that the hard way. I'm trying to learn it the easier way, by watching him.

We'll see if it works.

Bram Ossory's fall forced him to rely on others, a stark contrast to Isbet Voll's fiercely guarded secret.

XIII. The Tide Merchant's Patience

I once watched a glassblower named Petran sell his entire season's work to the autumn trader in a single afternoon—and then realize, too late, that he'd given it all away for far too little.

He knew it by November. By December, he was certain. By February, when word came back from the southern markets of what his work had sold for in the wealthy households Odalys supplied, he could calculate the loss down to the last copper piece — not a guess, not a suspicion, an actual number he could have put in his household ledger if he'd had the stomach to write it down. He didn't lose money, exactly. The autumn price Odalys paid was fair enough by the standards of a trader working on a fleet's fixed schedule. But he left a meaningful sum on the table — his own money, his own work's worth — because he couldn't stand the thought of finished glass sitting unsold through winter while his family needed income in hand.

The thing that bothered him most, he told me later, wasn't even the money itself. It was how predictable the whole mistake had been. He'd known, the morning Odalys's boats appeared in the harbor, that spring prices ran higher. Everyone in the Cinderquay knew it. But knowing a thing in your head and acting on it when your kiln's empty and your household's low on coin are two entirely different problems, and Petran — like most of the glassblowers on the harbor road — sold anyway, out of a fear that felt, in the moment it seized him, too urgent to argue with.

I'm dwelling on Petran's mistake because I want you to feel what that autumn decision point actually costs. Not as an abstract principle (patience pays, haste costs you, etc.) but as a real pressure most skilled people face at some point in their work: the gap between what you could get right now, today, in your hand, versus what your work might actually be worth if you could afford to wait for the buyer who values it properly. The gap is often wide. The ability to wait for the better offer, without your household depending on you closing the gap immediately, is one of the clearest dividing lines I know between work that eventually builds something durable and work that stays trapped in a cycle of selling too early, too cheaply, because the next month's expenses won't wait.

What would it have taken for Petran to hold back even a quarter of his best pieces?

I'm not answering that yet. Hold the question.

Every autumn, a coastal trader named Odalys — no relation to the glassblower of the same name I mentioned earlier in this book, though the name was common enough along that stretch of shore to cause occasional confusion — arrived in Ashmere's harbor with a small fleet, buying up finished glass to carry south where wealthier households paid premiums for anything from the Cinderquay's kilns. Her arrival was a small ritual in the quarter. The first sighting of her sails rounding the headland passed from workshop to workshop faster than almost any other news the quarter carried, and for two or three days each autumn the harbor road took on a different rhythm entirely — glassblowers who'd spent all season working toward this single window now pulling stock from shelves and storerooms, laying it out for her inspection with the nervous energy of people who understood, without saying so aloud, that missing this sale meant gambling on winter with no guaranteed buyer waiting on the other side.

I always found something faintly theatrical in the whole affair. Odalys walking the row with a practiced, unhurried air. Picking up a piece here, setting one down there. Naming a price with the flat confidence of someone who knew exactly how much urgency a closing season could extract from a nervous seller. And most sellers — however much they grumbled privately about her rates — selling to her anyway, because the alternative was unsold stock sitting through a long, cold, income-less winter, and that was a risk most households in the quarter simply could not afford to take.

Isbet Voll, whose blue by then had earned her a reputation that reached well beyond the local harbor markets, was the rare glassblower who did not sell to the autumn trader at all. Or rather, she sold only occasionally, and only a fraction of her finished stock — enough to keep her household steady through winter, but nowhere near the volume most of her neighbors moved in those few urgent autumn days. When a younger glassblower once asked her why she seemed to turn away easy custom every single year, Isbet gave an answer strange enough that the younger woman repeated it to me afterward, still puzzling over what it meant.

"Odalys buys at the price that suits her fleet's schedule," Isbet said, "not the price my glass is actually worth to the households she's selling it to. She's not a bad trader — I don't fault her for buying cheap when the market lets her. That's simply her trade, the same way mine is glass. But I've watched enough seasons now to know that if I hold even half my finished stock through winter and carry it myself to the spring fair, I'll sell it for nearly twice what her autumn price offers, to buyers who've had all winter to want something they can't get anywhere closer to home."

The younger glassblower — whose name I've lost to time, though I remember the skepticism in her voice clearly enough — pointed out the obvious risk. A winter's worth of finished glass, stored rather than sold, was glass that could crack in a cold snap, or gather dust, or simply fail to sell as well as hoped come spring. You could end up with nothing to show for all that patience except a workshop full of unsold pieces and a winter's worth of missed income you could have had in hand months earlier.

She wasn't wrong to raise it. A number of glassblowers who tried to imitate Isbet's practice in the years after it became more widely known did, in fact, come to grief with it — holding back stock they couldn't truly afford to hold, in seasons when their households needed the autumn income regardless of what a better spring price might eventually offer. I watched this happen more than once, and it was never pretty: a household betting everything on a price that never materialized, or a cold winter cracking half the held stock, or (worst of all) a glassblower so committed to imitating Isbet's patience that they refused an autumn sale even when their own family was eating thinner every week.

Isbet herself was careful, whenever a younger glassblower asked her advice, to draw a sharp distinction between what she was doing and what she saw the imitators attempting. "I'm not telling anyone to gamble everything on a better price," she said more than once, to more than one eager listener. "I'm telling you to hold back only what you can genuinely afford to lose entirely, and to sell the rest at whatever fair price the season offers, so your household never depends on the gamble succeeding. The people who get hurt imitating me are the ones who heard 'hold your stock' and forgot the much less exciting first half of the sentence, which is 'hold only what you can afford to.'"

This is the part most advice about patience leaves out, and I want to be blunt about it because the omission causes real damage: patience is not a virtue you practice with resources you actually need next month. Patience is what you do with the surplus, the margin, the portion of your work that your household can survive without if the waiting turns out badly. If you don't have that margin yet, your job is not to practice patience — your job is to build the margin first, by selling whatever you need to sell at whatever fair price the market offers, until you've earned enough room to start holding back the pieces that might fetch more later.

Isbet did not deny the risk. "It's a real risk," she told me once, "and I don't take it with everything I make. I sell enough through the winter markets and to Odalys both to keep my household steady regardless of how the spring fair goes. But whatever I can genuinely afford to hold, I hold, because I've learned that most glassblowers in this quarter sell out of fear rather than calculation. Afraid the piece in hand might crack before it sells. Afraid a slow season means a bad season. Afraid that turning down an easy buyer today means no buyer will come tomorrow. Most of the time that fear isn't telling them anything true about the market. It's only telling them something true about how uncomfortable it feels to wait."

I asked her once how she'd first arrived at this practice, since it ran against the habit of nearly every other glassblower on the harbor road. She told me it had begun almost by accident, in her second year of independent work, when a batch of her finest pieces simply weren't ready in time for Odalys's autumn arrival — still cooling in the Long Kiln when the trading boats departed for the season. Rather than lose the sale entirely, she'd carried the finished stock herself to the spring fair the following year, more out of necessity than strategy, and had been startled by how much more the pieces fetched from buyers who'd spent a whole winter wanting something they couldn't get any closer to home.

"I didn't plan the lesson," she said. "The lesson happened to me because my kiln was slow that year, and I was simply paying attention when it did."

Here's what I learned watching Isbet's practice hold across a number of years: in an ordinary season, the patience earned her roughly what she predicted — a meaningfully better price at the spring fair than Odalys's autumn rate would have given her. In one unusually hard winter, a portion of her held stock did in fact suffer, several pieces cracking from a cold spell that reached even the careful storage she kept them in, and she took a real loss on the gamble that year. A loss she admitted to readily when I asked about it.

I remember walking through her storeroom with her the morning after that particular cold snap broke. The quiet, businesslike way she catalogued what had survived and what hadn't. Setting the cracked pieces aside for remelting without any visible self-pity, the way a person handles a loss they'd genuinely accounted for in advance rather than one that caught them by surprise.

"I lost that year," she said plainly. "I don't pretend the patience always pays. What I've found, across enough years to trust the pattern rather than any single season of it, is that it pays more often than it fails, and by a wider margin when it succeeds than it costs me on the seasons it doesn't."

She paused, running her hand along the edge of a shelf that still held pieces that had made it through intact.

"A merchant who sells everything the moment a buyer appears, out of fear the buyer might be the only one who ever comes, will never discover whether a better buyer was two seasons away the whole time. I'd rather know that, even on the years it costs me something to find out."

There was a particular spring fair, some years into this pattern, that Isbet described to me as the clearest vindication of her whole approach. A wealthy household from far up the coast — having heard secondhand of her blue but never having seen it in person — sent a steward the full distance specifically to attend the fair, on the understanding that no closer market carried it reliably. The steward arrived with a standing offer generous enough that Isbet sold nearly her whole winter's held stock within the fair's first morning, at prices well beyond even her own optimistic expectations.

She told me afterward that she'd thought, watching the steward count out the coin, of every autumn she'd turned Odalys away for a fraction of that same sum.

"I don't think that household would ever have traveled so far for glass they could simply buy from a passing trading boat in October," she said. "The waiting wasn't incidental to what they were willing to pay. In a strange way, it was part of what they were paying for."

The trader Odalys herself, for her part, never seemed to hold Isbet's habit against her. The two women maintained an easy, businesslike friendship across the years despite selling to each other so rarely. I asked Odalys once, on one of her autumn visits to the cove, what she made of Isbet's practice.

She laughed — not unkindly.

"She's right about my price, of course. I buy at the rate my own fleet's schedule demands, not at whatever a piece might eventually fetch from someone willing to wait for it. I don't take it personally. I'd do the same in her position, if patience were a thing my own trade allowed me to practice. But a fleet has to sail on the tide it has, not the tide it wishes it had. And Isbet is fortunate enough to answer to nobody's schedule but her own."

That last phrase stuck with me: *fortunate enough to answer to nobody's schedule but her own.*

Is that fortune, or is it something Isbet built deliberately, year by year, by selling just enough to keep her household steady and holding back just enough to test whether the market would eventually pay her what her work was actually worth?

I think the distinction matters more than it seems to at first. Because if you believe patience is a luxury only lucky people can afford, you'll never build the margin that makes patience possible in the first place. But if you understand that the margin is something you construct — by selling what you must, saving what you can, and testing the waiting in small enough increments that a failed test doesn't sink you — then patience stops being a gamble and starts being a practice you can actually learn.

Petran, the glassblower I opened this chapter with, did eventually learn it. It took him three more seasons of watching Isbet's practice hold, and one very hard conversation with his own household about what they could genuinely afford to do without for a winter, but he learned it. The next autumn, when Odalys's boats appeared, he sold her half his finished stock and held the rest. Not because he was suddenly braver or less afraid of the risk. Because he'd done the arithmetic carefully enough to know that even if every held piece cracked, his household would survive the winter on what he'd already sold, and that was enough room to find out whether the fear that had cost him money every prior season was measuring anything real.

It wasn't. The spring fair paid him nearly double what Odalys's autumn rate would have. He came back from that fair and told me, with a mix of relief and frustration I understood completely, that he'd been leaving that money on the table every single year, not because he couldn't afford to wait, but because he'd never once stopped to calculate whether he could.

What are you selling right now — your work, your time, your attention — at the first offer, because you can't stand the discomfort of waiting to see what it might actually be worth?

The unmarked blue held more than just pigment – it contained a legacy, and Corra Fenn knew that some ledgers hold more than cracks.

XIV. The Glass That Remembers

I was standing at the Long Kiln's cooling bench the afternoon Joset Corvane brought in the magistrate's commission pieces, and I knew instantly something wasn't right.

The magistrate's pieces had cooled perfectly, flawlessly even—but I knew, with a sickening certainty, that the perfection itself was a deception. The glass hadn't simply *cooled* evenly; it had been rushed, forced to solidify before its internal stresses could resolve themselves.

I told him no anyway. He didn't argue. He just thanked me, took the pieces to someone less careful, and six months later a third of them shattered in a dining hall three towns off during the coldest week of winter.

Glass carries what the trade calls memory. Not metaphorically. Actually. A piece shaped under stress and cooled too quickly doesn't just look fine for a while before it fails — it carries, in its molecular structure, a kind of tension, a record of the shortcut that made it, and given the right conditions months or years later, it will try to return to the shape it wanted to be before you rushed it into something else. The annealing kiln's job isn't to make glass pretty. It's to let the piece forget, slowly enough that the forgetting holds.

I did not know, watching Joset leave with those pieces, that I was watching the same principle play out in a man.

Joset apprenticed two workshops down from mine during my own middle years at the Cinderquay, and for his first six years working independently he was the most gifted and least trustworthy glassblower on the harbor road. Gifted because pieces coming off his pipe had a liveliness older, more methodical hands openly envied. Untrustworthy because he pulled work from the annealing furnace early more consistently than anyone I'd watched in forty years, on the theory that his own eye could judge a finished piece better than a rule written by men who'd never seen him work.

He wasn't being reckless the way an outsider might assume. He genuinely believed his talent had earned him an exception. And for six years, buyers who didn't yet know his name kept commissioning him precisely because his rushed pieces looked as good as anything Isbet Voll or Corliss Fen ever produced on the Long Kiln's full patient schedule. The trouble showed itself later, in kitchens three towns off, in pieces that cracked at a season's remove for reasons no one standing there could see.

The magistrate's commission — the full set of forty I turned away — ended that run. Not immediately. The pieces were delivered on time to real acclaim. Joset went on believing his reputation intact for nearly a year. Then the magistrate's letter arrived, demanding restitution Joset could barely afford, and I watched what that letter did to him.

He came to the Long Kiln the week after it landed and asked, plainly, if I would teach him the discipline properly. The way my father taught me, not the way six years of unearned confidence had taught him to ignore it.

I agreed. I did not expect the change to hold.

I had watched enough gifted, chastened young men promise reform in the week after a costly failure to know how easily the promise fades once the shame cools. But Joset's reform held. For ten years. He tested every unfamiliar batch. Honored every full cooling schedule. Turned down two separate rushed commissions at real cost to himself. Built, across that patient decade, a reputation nearly as steady as Isbet Voll's own. Spoken of as a cautionary tale reversed — the gifted young man who actually learned the lesson rather than just surviving the failure that taught it.

I annealed for him across those ten years without a single irregular request. By the decade's end I had quietly stopped thinking of him as a man who needed watching.

You might be thinking that's proof enough. Ten years of clean work, of discipline held under ordinary pressure, of commissions turned down when the timeline didn't allow for proper cooling. Ten years ought to mean the old shortcut is gone, replaced entirely by the new habit. That's what I thought, standing at the Long Kiln watching Joset's pieces come through on schedule, month after month, year after year.

The glass knew better.

The strain that found Joset again, in his eleventh reformed year, came from a direction that had nothing to do with the furnace. His youngest daughter — she was seven, I knew her from the harbor road, bright kid, used to sit on the workshop steps watching him work — fell seriously ill. Fever that settled in her chest and would not lift. The healer treating her named a costly imported remedy as the best chance of pulling her through, a sum Joset didn't have and couldn't raise, in the time the healer said mattered, through ordinary trade at its ordinary pace.

A wealthy household on the harbor road, hearing of his trouble, offered him a commission. Generous terms. Single condition: finished within the week.

For a simple piece, the timeline would've been comfortable. For what they actually wanted — an ambitious set, the kind of work that built Joset's early reputation — it was exactly the kind of pressure his old habit had thrived under.

I didn't know any of this when he brought the pieces to the Long Kiln that week. He didn't tell me about his daughter. Didn't mention the deadline or what was riding on it. Just asked, the way any glassblower asks, for the standard annealing schedule. And when I looked at the pieces and saw they needed the full time — no shortcuts, no exceptions — I refused the early pull the same way I'd refused Corliss Fen's goblets forty years earlier.

He didn't argue. He thanked me and left.

What I learned later, from his own account and from his wife: he took the pieces to a private kiln at the edge of the quarter. Half-abandoned place, used to belong to a retired glassblower, stood mostly empty. He finished the annealing there himself, a full day short of what the pieces needed, telling himself the entire time that ten years of discipline had finally earned him the judgment to know which single exception was safe to make.

The pieces held long enough to be delivered. Long enough to be paid for. Long enough to buy the remedy that pulled his daughter through the fever. And I want to be honest about something here: I have never once heard Joset express regret over that particular choice, whatever the pieces themselves eventually did. A man measuring his daughter's life against a stranger's serving glass is not measuring in the same currency this book has been weighing for thirteen stories.

But the pieces cracked. Three of the twelve. Within the season. In the buyer's own dining hall during an ordinary supper. And the story traveled the harbor road with the speed a fallen reputation always travels faster than a rising one.

Here's what I need you to feel before I tell you what happened next.

The buyer had commissioned those pieces in good faith. Paid honestly. Set them on their table expecting the quality Joset's reformed reputation promised. They were sitting at supper — family, probably guests, the kind of evening you set good glass out for — when the first piece went. Not dropped. Not knocked. Just cracked, stem to bowl, while someone was holding it. Then another. Then a third. In front of people. The kind of failure that doesn't just cost you the piece. It costs you the evening, the embarrassment, the quiet knowledge that you paid premium prices for work that couldn't hold.

That's the cost Joset's desperate exception actually carried. Not to him — his daughter lived, and I genuinely don't think he'd change that trade — but to someone three towns off who had no idea they were buying glass shaped in the middle of someone else's crisis.

Joset came to me after the pieces' failure reached him. Stood in the Long Kiln's doorway the way he'd stood there eleven years before, the week of the magistrate's letter. But he looked different this time. Less ashamed than genuinely bewildered.

"I don't understand it," he said. "I haven't rushed a piece in eleven years. Standing at that old kiln, I didn't feel like the man who once rushed forty pieces for a magistrate. I felt like a father buying his daughter a chance. I don't know how the same hands that held the line for a decade found their way back to the exact shortcut I thought I'd unlearned entirely."

I told him what I'd told him once before, though neither of us had fully understood it the first time.

Glass that's been shaped and cooled properly doesn't forget the strain of its first, hastier shaping just because it's since been annealed correctly. The memory sits in it regardless. Quiet. Undetectable under ordinary conditions. It's only under a stress sharp enough to reach that deeper layer — a stress the ordinary years never happened to apply — that the old shape reasserts itself. Not because the annealing failed. Because the annealing was never actually erasing the memory. It was only holding it still.

A man's habits carry the same property. I didn't have language for it until I watched Joset's decade collapse under a single week's genuine desperation. Ten years of honest discipline hadn't erased the shortcut his first six years carved into him. It had only kept that shortcut quiet under the ordinary pressures a working life usually applies. And it took a pressure of an entirely different order — not a tight deadline for its own sake, but his child's life set against it — to reach down to the layer the ordinary decade had never been tested against.

I'm telling you this not to excuse what happened to that buyer's dining hall. They lost pieces they paid honestly for and deserved better. I'm telling you because I think it's the truest thing this book can say about reform of any kind: a habit set aside is not a habit erased. The years that pass without it resurfacing are not proof it's gone. Only proof that nothing yet has pressed hard enough, in exactly the old direction, to find it still there.

Think about your own business for a minute. The shortcut you used to take when you were scrambling — the corner you cut on vetting, on due diligence, on the quiet discipline that separates a sustainable decision from an expedient one. Maybe you stopped taking it. Maybe it's been years. Maybe you've built a whole second reputation on the steadier work that replaced it, the way Joset built his reformed decade, and you've started to trust that the old version of yourself is gone, replaced entirely by the person you've been proving yourself to be, month after month, under normal conditions.

What happens when the conditions stop being normal?

What happens when the pressure arrives from a direction you didn't see coming — not another tight deadline you can white-knuckle through, but something that reweights the whole equation, something that makes the old shortcut feel, in the moment, not like a compromise but like the only rational choice available to you? Your own equivalent of Joset's daughter. The thing that makes you feel, standing there, not like someone backsliding into an old habit but like someone making a hard, clear-eyed decision under circumstances the ordinary rule was never written to account for.

The glass remembers.

Joset rebuilt a second time. More slowly than the first. He told me once, late in that second rebuilding, that he'd stopped believing any number of clean years could fully retire the old shortcut. And he'd made a private rule considerably stranger than any this book has offered before it.

On the weeks he felt most desperate — most certain his own judgment could be trusted past the ordinary rule — he brought every piece to the Long Kiln and asked me, specifically, to hold it the full time myself. Not because he didn't trust his own hands under normal pressure. Because he'd learned that the weeks he felt most capable of judging the exception were exactly the weeks the old shape was closest to the surface. The memory pressing hardest against the annealing that had, for years, held it still.

I think about that rule more than I think about any other discipline this book has named. Because it's not a rule about avoiding failure. It's a rule built on the assumption that the old failure is still there, waiting, and that the clearest sign it's about to surface is the feeling of absolute certainty that this time, just this once, you can see the safe exception the ordinary rule was never meant to forbid.

Which brings me to the question I haven't answered yet, the one I need you to hold a little longer before we're done.

If the annealing never actually erases the memory — if ten years of discipline only holds the old shortcut quiet without removing it — then what's the point of the reform at all? Why spend a decade building a steadier practice if the first real pressure is going to find the old shape still there, ready to reassert itself the moment the stakes are high enough to make the shortcut feel, once again, like the rational choice?

I'll tell you what I told Joset, standing at the Long Kiln the week he brought me that private rule.

The point isn't to believe the old habit is gone. The point is to know exactly where it still lives, and to build your disciplines not around the assumption that you've outgrown it, but around the knowledge that you haven't. The rule that actually holds isn't "I don't do that anymore." It's "I know I'm most likely to do that again on the weeks I'm most certain I can judge the exception, so those are the weeks I remove the judgment from my own hands entirely."

That's not the reform failing. That's the reform finally understanding what it's up against.

Even the keeper of cracks understood that every piece held a story—and Eleanor Voss was about to learn what happens when those stories collide.

XV. The Common Purse

Rurik Bellwright stood in the rain outside what used to be his workshop, staring at a single, jagged crack that ran clean through the hearth of his furnace—a fissure that mirrored the fracture within his livelihood.

It ran the full width of his furnace hearth. Clean through. The kind of break that doesn't come from careless banking or an unsupervised apprentice or any of the fifty careful habits he'd built his reputation on across two decades of work along the Cinderquay. The lightning had traveled down through the dead tree at the edge of his property—the one he'd been meaning to fell for three seasons now, always next month, always when he had the time—and straight into the ground beneath his foundation.

The stone had split like kindling.

His apprentice stood beside him, silent. The rain was getting harder. Rurik realized, standing there, that he had no idea what happened next. Not in any practical sense. He had eleven years of savings in a strongbox upstairs, which sounded like a great deal until you did the math on rebuilding a furnace hearth at the height of the season with no income coming in to replace what you were spending, and he had a household that depended on the workshop staying open, and he had—

He had refused, every autumn for eleven years, to pay into the one fund that existed to cover exactly this.

I'm starting with Rurik in the rain because I want you to feel what he felt in that moment before I explain how he got there. That sick drop in your stomach when you realize the position you've been standing in for years—the position that felt so solid, so well-reasoned, so different from the careless way other people ran their lives—just became the position that's going to ruin you.

And you can't undo it by being more careful tomorrow.

The fund Rurik had refused still exists. It's kept among the masters of the Cinderquay even now, small and unglamorous and rarely discussed outside the quarter itself. Every established workshop pays a modest sum each season. Out of it, any workshop that loses its furnace room entirely—to fire, to storm, to the particular catastrophe a trade built around open flame is never fully insured against by care alone—draws enough to rebuild rather than fold.

When the quarter's masters first proposed it, Rurik objected. Loudly.

"I bank my own coal each night the way my master taught me," he said at the meeting where the proposal was debated in the square. Several people who were there that afternoon repeated this to me years later, word for word, with the particular precision people reserve for arguments they wish they'd thought of first. "I do not leave a lamp burning near my sand stores. I do not let an apprentice work a furnace unsupervised past dusk. If another workshop burns from its own carelessness, I do not see why my own careful decades should be taxed to rebuild it."

A number of the quarter's more careful masters found this persuasive. The purse very nearly failed.

Here's what I want you to notice about Rurik's reasoning, because I have heard versions of it in every industry I've ever worked in, and I have watched it ruin people who were genuinely competent at their trade:

He was not wrong about his own carefulness.

His workshop *was* more carefully run than most. He *did* bank his coal correctly. He *did* supervise his apprentices. In eleven years, his workshop never had so much as a scorched beam, while three other workshops in that same stretch drew on the purse for genuine misfortunes entirely outside their control.

The problem was not that Rurik was careless. The problem was that he thought his carefulness was the same thing as safety, and it isn't. It never has been.

Self-sufficiency is a story you tell yourself about why disaster happens to other people. Safety is what you have when you stop telling that story and start preparing for the disaster that doesn't care about your discipline at all.

Do you see the difference? It's not semantic. It's the difference between Rurik standing in his intact workshop each autumn, turning away the fund collector with a rehearsed speech about his own standards, and Rurik standing in the rain staring at a crack his standards had nothing to do with, realizing he'd spent eleven years building a position with no margin for being wrong.

Because that's what he'd actually been doing, all those years. Not protecting his workshop. Protecting his story about himself.

Every season that passed without disaster made the story a little more solid. A little more weight-bearing. Until he could stand his whole sense of security on top of it without feeling it shift under his feet. The fund collector would knock each autumn. Rurik would explain, again, about his discipline and his standards and his strongbox. And the story would grow another ring, like a tree, until it was thick enough that he couldn't see through it anymore to the simple fact that lightning doesn't check your banking habits before it strikes your property.

You might be thinking: But he was right to be careful. His carefulness did protect him for eleven years.

And yes. It did. But here's what I need you to understand, because this is the part that wrecks people:

The protection his carefulness gave him was real. It was just protecting him from a completely different category of disaster than the one that finally found him. And the entire time he was standing inside his carefully-built fortress congratulating himself on his discipline, he was leaving himself completely exposed to the tree he kept meaning to fell and never got around to, the lightning strike no amount of banked coal would prevent, the crack through the hearth that had nothing to do with how well he'd trained his apprentices.

The disaster that ends you is almost never the one you spent years preparing for. It's the one that came from the direction you weren't looking, because you were too busy looking at the people around you who were less careful than you and assuming that the gap between their carelessness and your discipline was the gap that mattered.

It isn't.

Isbet Voll understood this. She was the one who tipped the original meeting toward establishing the fund in the first place, after listening to Rurik's speech about banking coal and supervising apprentices.

"Care protects against carelessness," she said, in the plain tone she used for most things. "It has never once protected against bad luck. And bad luck is the only thing this purse is actually meant to cover."

She paused. Then added something I didn't understand the weight of until years later: "I have never once heard of a fire in the Cinderquay's whole recorded history that began with a careless hand rather than an unlucky one. A coal popping further than any banking could have predicted. A lightning strike. A spark carried by wind from a neighbor's chimney onto a roof no one on that particular property had any hand in shingling."

The fund was established. Rurik refused to pay into it. For eleven years.

And I want to be clear about what those eleven years cost him, because the cost was not something you could tally in coin at the time. It was subtler than that. What Rurik lost, across those eleven years of refusal, was the capacity to be wrong at a recoverable scale.

Think about that for a moment.

When you build a position that depends entirely on your own discipline, your own savings, your own strongbox full of careful choices, you are also building a position where a single mistake—or a single piece of bad luck you mistake for someone else's mistake—can end you. There's no give in the system. No room to say, two seasons in, "I think I misunderstood what I was protecting myself against," and adjust your position while you still have the margin to do so without begging.

Rurik didn't have that room anymore. By the time the lightning struck, he was either right about everything he'd believed for eleven years, or he was ruined. Those were his options. And the tree didn't care which one he preferred.

I was present at the masters' meeting called the week after the storm to decide what, if anything, the quarter owed a man who had refused for over a decade to pay into the very fund he now desperately needed.

The room was divided. Sharply.

Several masters argued—and not unreasonably—that a fund isn't a fund at all if it can be joined the moment it's needed and ignored every season it isn't. That paying Rurik out of a purse he'd spent eleven years refusing to feed would teach every other workshop in the quarter that the fund's rules meant nothing once genuine hardship arrived.

Grethe Vane, who had drawn on the fund herself two years prior after a chimney fire no one could have predicted, said something I've never forgotten: "If we pay him now, we are teaching the whole quarter that the only insurance worth buying is the kind you can purchase retroactively, after you already know what broke."

I thought that was going to carry the room.

But Isbet argued the opposite position. The harder side of it.

"The purse was never built to reward the careful and punish the unlucky," she said. "It was built because bad luck does not check a man's contribution history before it strikes his hearth. If we let Rurik's household go under this winter to prove a point about fairness, we will have built a fund that protects everyone except the one man arrogant enough to think he never needed it—which is precisely the man a genuine misfortune is most likely to find unprepared."

She paused. Looked around the room. Then said, quieter: "And if we are willing to watch one workshop fall to teach the rest of the quarter a lesson about obedience, I do not think we have built a fund against bad luck at all. I think we have built a fund against people we don't like."

The quarter settled, in the end, on a compromise that satisfied no one fully and has become the purse's quiet precedent ever since.

Rurik received half what a full contributor would have drawn. Enough to rebuild his hearth and resume his trade within the season rather than lose the whole of it. But considerably less than the workshops that had paid faithfully for the same eleven years. And he was required, from that season forward, to pay not only his ordinary share but a modest additional sum each season for a further decade—what the quarter came to call, half-jokingly and half in earnest, his back debt to luck he never thought he owed.

Rurik paid it. Every season. For the whole of that decade. Without complaint.

And he became, in his later years, the fund's most vocal defender to any new workshop along the harbor road tempted toward his old reasoning.

"I thought I was insuring myself against my neighbors' carelessness," he told a young glassblower once. The young man repeated the conversation to me afterward, and I've thought about it more times than I can count. "I have come to understand that no one is actually insuring against carelessness at all, careful or otherwise. Every one of us is insuring against the one piece of bad luck our own care was never built to catch, because it never occurs to a careful man to guard against a kind of misfortune his own carefulness has nothing to do with."

He looked at the young man for a long moment. Then said: "I spent eleven years believing my discipline made me safer than my neighbors. It made me safer than nothing at all, in the one direction the lightning actually came from."

What I want you to take from Rurik's story is not that discipline doesn't matter. It does. His careful habits protected his workshop for eleven years from the kinds of disasters that careful habits actually prevent. That's real. That's worth doing.

But here's the piece I think he paid too much to learn, and the piece I hope you can learn more cheaply:

The disaster that will end you is not going to come from the direction you've been guarding. It's going to come from the direction you couldn't see because you were standing inside a story about your own preparedness that had no room in it for the tree you kept meaning to fell. For the lightning that strikes careful people exactly as hard as it strikes careless ones. For the crack through the hearth that discipline has no power over at all.

And the way you prepare for that disaster is not by being more careful. It's by admitting, out loud and in practical terms, that you do not know which direction the lightning is coming from, and paying into the systems that exist to catch you when it strikes from the direction your carefulness wasn't facing.

That's what the common purse actually is. Not a tax on competence paid to cover someone else's carelessness. A plain acknowledgment that some of the things that will break your workshop in the years to come are things you will never see coming, and the coin you pay each season is the price of being wrong without being ruined.

The people I have watched make Rurik's mistake, in the years since—and I have watched many—have almost never been careless people. They've been people who believed their own discipline made them safer than it actually did. Who looked at the mutual aid, the safety nets, the common funds they were invited to join before they needed them, and saw a tax on their competence rather than insurance against the unforeseeable.

And the misfortune that found them was never the kind they'd been guarding against. It was always the tree. The thing they didn't see coming because their discipline had taught them to see only the disasters that discipline prevents, and they'd mistaken that limited vision for comprehensive safety.

So here is the question Rurik's story leaves you with. Not whether you're careful enough to avoid needing help. You're probably very careful. That's not what's going to save you.

The question is whether you're building the kind of position that lets you be wrong—about anything, ever—without losing everything at once. Whether the systems you're refusing to pay into now, because you believe your discipline makes you exempt from the misfortunes they cover, are actually covering the things your discipline has no power over at all.

Because the tree is already there, at the edge of your property. You just haven't noticed it yet. And when the lightning comes, it won't matter how carefully you banked your coal last night. It will only matter whether you built a position where being wrong about one thing means losing everything, or whether you paid into the fund that exists specifically to catch the disaster your carefulness was never designed to see.

Rurik rebuilt his hearth. Paid his back debt for a decade. Spent the rest of his working life trying to teach the people coming up behind him the difference between discipline and safety, between self-sufficiency and the kind of position that leaves you no room to be wrong without begging.

He learned it. But he learned it standing in the rain, looking at the crack, with no good options left.

You don't have to learn it that way. The fund is there. The question is whether you'll pay into it while you still have the margin to be wrong, or whether you'll wait until being wrong is the only option you have left.

The common purse operates on a logic most people were never taught to see. You were raised on self-reliance. Savings. Planning. Being the kind of person who doesn't need to ask. And all of that is fine until the thing that breaks you isn't a failure of character but a failure of arithmetic—until the gap between what you can save alone and what catastrophe actually costs becomes wide enough to swallow you whole.

The common purse isn't built for the disasters you can see coming. It's built for the ones you can't. The medical bill that's three times what the insurance said. The lawsuit from the accident that wasn't your fault but is somehow your problem. The month your car, your roof, and your child's school fees all decide to fail in the same two-week span, as though synchronized by some cosmic sense of humor.

What savings lets you survive is misfortune. What the common purse lets you survive is *compounding* misfortune—the thing that happens when bad luck doesn't arrive politely, one catastrophe at a time, but comes in overlapping waves that drain you faster than you can rebuild.

Here's the part that sounds wrong until you see it: the common purse makes you *less* vulnerable than self-sufficiency, even when you're the one paying in more than you're taking out. Because what you're buying isn't a refund. You're buying the ability to take risks that self-sufficient people can't afford. You're buying the clearance to make the job change, start the business, move to the new city, take the relationship seriously—all the decisions that hinge not on "can I do this?" but on "can I survive being wrong about this?"

The people outside the system think they're freer. They're not answerable to anyone. They owe nothing. They stand alone. And they do—right up until standing alone means standing still, because every meaningful decision is also a gamble they can't afford to lose.

The people inside the system have a different kind of freedom. They can be wrong. They can try the thing that might not work. They can take the chance that has real upside but also real downside, because the downside doesn't mean annihilation—it means falling into a net they helped weave when their hands were steady.

That's the thing the purely self-reliant never calculate: how much of their life is spent avoiding risk not because the risk is bad but because they couldn't survive the loss. How many opportunities never even register as opportunities because the question isn't "would this be worth it?" but "could I get back up if it didn't work?"

The common purse isn't charity. It's not a handout system for the careless subsidized by the responsible. It's a structure that says: *we all live in a world where being careful isn't enough.* Where the margin between doing everything right and losing everything anyway is thinner than your monthly income. Where the distance between "I'm fine" and "I'm not fine" is one uninsured week in the ICU, one flooded basement, one mistake you didn't even make but got billed for anyway.

And the buy-in isn't generosity. It's math. It's the recognition that the cost of building the net when you don't need it is smaller than the cost of needing it when it doesn't exist.

XVI. The Cheap Winter's Wood

I remember the exact afternoon Maren Holt made the purchase that half the Cinderquay thought would ruin her – she bought enough wood for an entire winter without haggling.

It was late February, the kind of raw wet cold that makes you question whether spring will ever actually come, and I was standing near the wood merchant's yard watching her inspect cord after cord of seasoned oak, running her hand along the grain, checking for the telltale signs of proper drying that every glassblower learns to read but most, by that point in the winter, had stopped bothering to check. The wood was good. Everyone knew the wood was good. The question that winter wasn't quality—it was whether anyone in their right mind would spend their savings on two years' worth of anything when the previous two years had taught the entire quarter that caution, not investment, was what kept a workshop alive.

The merchant, a man named Torben Vass who'd been supplying the Cinderquay's furnaces for longer than I'd been watching them, wasn't even trying to sell hard anymore. He'd dropped his price three times already that season, and the glassblowers had stayed away regardless, and by the time Maren showed up with her coin purse and her tape measure, I think he'd mostly resigned himself to eating the loss and trying again next year with whatever was left. When she told him she wanted two full years of wood, delivered and stacked, he actually asked her to repeat herself. Not because he hadn't heard. Because he wanted to be sure, before he accepted, that she understood what she was doing.

She understood. What I don't think Vass understood, or what most of her neighbors along that stretch of workshops understood either, was that Maren had spent the previous two lean years asking herself a different question than everyone else was asking. They were asking: how little can I spend and still keep working? She was asking: what does a furnace actually need, regardless of what the market thinks it needs right now?

The difference between those two questions is the difference between surviving a hard season and positioning yourself to win the season that comes after it. But here's the trouble: you can't tell which question someone's asking just by watching them work through lean times. Caution and strategy look identical in February when wood is cheap and no one's buying. It's only later, when the market turns, that you find out whether someone was being prudent or whether they were just scared.

Most of the Cinderquay, that winter, was scared. And I don't mean that as criticism. Two years of thin work does something to your decision-making that's hard to describe if you haven't lived through it yourself. It's not that you stop thinking clearly—it's that your definition of "clear thinking" shifts, gradually and then all at once, until the only measure of good judgment you can still trust is whether you're holding onto your coin harder than you were yesterday. Spending starts to feel reckless by definition. Saving starts to feel like the only responsible choice, regardless of what's actually for sale or what it's selling for.

The wood merchants, meanwhile, were in their own version of the same trap. They'd overstocked two years earlier, betting on a recovery that never quite materialized, and now they were sitting on more seasoned fuel than the quarter's cautious glassblowers were willing to burn through. Basic supply and demand pushed the price down, first a little, then a lot. By midwinter you could buy a cord of properly dried oak—wood that would've cost you sixty silver two years earlier—for twenty-three.

Everyone saw the same falling price. What they read into it was different.

Most read it as confirmation that the whole trade was still weakening, that worse was coming, that a smart glassblower should hold tight and spend nothing beyond what each week's immediate work demanded. Maren read it as a temporary mismatch between what something cost and what it was actually worth. The oak hadn't gotten worse. The furnaces hadn't started needing less fuel. Fear had made the price collapse, and fear, in her view, was a terrible guide to value but an excellent guide to opportunity.

You might be thinking: that's just hindsight talking. Maren got lucky, a storm hit, and now we're all supposed to pretend she was smart instead of fortunate.

Fair enough. Let me tell you what happened to the glassblowers who didn't buy.

When the storm came—and I'll get to the storm in a minute, because the storm matters, but it's not actually the point—the wood supply across the entire harbor contracted so fast that workshops all along the Cinderquay found themselves, for the first time in living memory, rationing furnace hours. Not because the market was slow. Because they literally could not afford enough fuel to keep their kilns running at normal capacity.

I watched Finn Crale, who ran a mid-sized workshop three doors down from Maren's, stand in the merchant's yard that April with his coin purse open, trying to buy a single week's worth of wood at triple the price he'd been used to paying, and Vass couldn't even sell it to him at that rate because a dozen other workshops had gotten there first and cleared out what little supply was left. Finn ended up running his furnace two days a week instead of six. Two days a week. Do you know what that does to a glassblower's income? It doesn't cut it by two-thirds. It cuts it further than that, because your best clients don't wait around for you to get back to full capacity—they find someone who never lost it.

Maren's furnace, meanwhile, ran seven days a week, full heat, no interruption, the entire spring. While Finn was running ads in the market square promising his clients he'd be back to normal production "as soon as supply stabilizes," Maren was working overtime filling the orders those clients placed with her instead.

That's the cost no one talks about when they talk about "being cautious with your savings." You think you're protecting yourself. What you're actually doing, in a moment when everyone around you is protecting themselves the exact same way, is guaranteeing that when the moment passes, you'll be starting from behind while someone else—someone who spent when you saved—is already running at full strength.

Let me be more specific about what Finn lost, because this is where the math gets cruel.

He saved, that winter, maybe two hundred silver by not buying wood he didn't immediately need. Prudent, right? Responsible financial management during uncertain times. But when spring came and he couldn't run his furnace, he lost approximately forty silver a week in income he would have earned at full capacity. Multiply that across twelve weeks—because it took that long for the supply situation to normalize—and he lost four hundred and eighty silver by being careful with two hundred.

Maren, meanwhile, spent about eleven hundred silver that winter on wood most of her neighbors thought she was foolish to buy. The same spring scarcity that cost Finn four hundred and eighty in lost income earned Maren nearly eight hundred in additional contracts from clients who couldn't wait for their usual suppliers to get back online. She didn't just avoid the loss. She captured the gain. And the gap between those two outcomes—Finn down four-eighty, Maren up eight hundred—isn't a gap you close by working harder once the crisis passes. That's a gap that compounds.

I want to pause here and tell you something I've never quite figured out how to say cleanly, which is that watching Finn realize what had happened—watching him stand in the square that June and do the math in his head, the math I just did for you—was one of the more uncomfortable things I've witnessed in thirty years of watching the Cinderquay's glassblowers navigate their trade. It wasn't that he'd made a bad decision in some reckless, obviously foolish way. It was that he'd made exactly the decision most sensible people in his position would've made, and it had cost him more than a year's careless spending could have.

The discipline Maren practiced that winter wasn't courage. I don't think courage is the right word for it at all. It was something harder to name: the ability to hold two ideas in her head simultaneously without letting one collapse into the other. The first idea was that two lean years had been real, that caution was warranted, that spending your savings on a guess could absolutely ruin you if the guess was wrong. The second idea was that wood's value to a furnace had not changed just because wood's price had temporarily crashed, and that a crashed price, in the right circumstances, wasn't a warning—it was an invitation.

Most people can hold one of those ideas clearly. Holding both, at the same time, while everyone around you is confidently holding only the first? That's the part that separates Maren from Finn. Not talent. Not luck. Just the ability to ask, while fear is still thick in the air and everyone's certain the fear is justified: has anything fundamental changed about what I actually need, or has only the price changed?

Here's the question I still don't have a clean answer to: can that actually be taught? Maren's old master—a woman named Solla Verin, stern as winter stone and about as warm—told me once that she'd spent the years after watching Maren's bet pay off trying to teach her own apprentices the same principle, and that she'd mostly failed. "They understand it when I explain it," she said. "They nod, they take notes, they say it back to me in their own words to prove they've got it. Then the next hard season comes and they save instead of spend anyway, because saving feels safe and spending feels like gambling, and no amount of me standing there telling them the difference between a real gamble and a mispriced certainty makes the spending feel less like gambling while they're the ones holding the purse."

I think about that a lot. The difference between understanding a principle and having the stomach to act on it while the circumstances that make it correct are still making everyone around you certain you're wrong.

The storm itself, since I've mentioned it twice now and ought to actually describe it: an early April squall, unusually fierce, tore through the forested hills east of Ashmere where most of the region's timber came from. Felled trees, flooded cuttings, roads washed out, the whole supply chain broken at once. The region had already been cutting less during the two lean years—less demand meant less harvest—and when the storm hit, the standing supply couldn't absorb the shock. Wood prices across the harbor tripled in a month.

But here's the thing I want you to hear clearly: Maren did not predict the storm. She told me that herself, years later, when I asked her point-blank whether she'd seen it coming. "If I'd known a storm was coming," she said, "I'd have bought four years of wood, not two, and rented a second shed. I didn't know anything except that a furnace needs what it needs regardless of what the market's mood is, and that the market's mood that winter was frightened enough to make the wood cheaper than the furnace's need could justify for long."

She would've looked just as foolish, she pointed out, if no storm had come and the wood had sat aging in her shed while her savings sat locked doing nothing. The fact that the storm came and vindicated her doesn't mean she was smart to bet on it. It means she was smart to bet that price and worth aren't the same measurement, and that a market frightened enough will eventually misprice something badly enough that the risk of buying becomes smaller than the risk of waiting.

What are you not buying right now because everyone around you has decided it's too expensive, or too risky, or too uncertain to spend on while things still feel unsettled?

I'm not asking what you should buy. I'm asking whether you've asked yourself the question Maren asked: has the thing's actual value to you changed, or has only its price changed because fear made it temporarily cheap? Because if it's the second, and you're waiting for the fear to lift before you buy, you're not being prudent. You're just guaranteeing you'll pay the high price later instead of the low price now.

The glassblowers who waited, that winter, didn't save themselves from risk. They simply transferred the risk from the decision to buy to the decision to wait, and when the wait cost them more than the purchase would have, they called it bad luck instead of what it actually was: the cost of letting fear decide what's valuable.

XVII. The Hands Not His Own

The ladder slipped on a patch of wet slate. Bram Ossory fell twelve feet, landed badly, and heard three distinct cracks in his right hand before the pain arrived.

He was fifty-three years old. He had spent thirty of those years running a stemware workshop at the Cinderquay's western edge, engraving every single piece himself—first gather to final polish, no exceptions—and he had just broken the hand that his entire reputation depended on.

The injury itself isn't the story. What matters is what Bram did in the four months that followed, when his hand wouldn't hold a finishing tool steady enough to cut the pattern he'd spent three decades perfecting, and every commissioned piece sat waiting in his workshop like an accusation.

Most people, hearing this, assume the lesson is about delegation. Or humility. Or learning to let go.

It's not.

The lesson is about what happens when you build something valuable entirely inside your own capacity to execute it, call that constraint a principle, and never once test whether the thing you're protecting is actually as fragile as you've convinced yourself it is.

I want to describe Bram's work first, because you need to understand what he thought he was protecting.

His stemware wasn't just competent. It was instantly recognizable. Each goblet carried a spiraling vine engraved freehand along the stem—no molds, no stencils, nothing mechanical—and the line had a particular quality buyers along the harbor road learned to spot from across a merchant's table. Not perfect. Alive. The vine seemed to move under your thumb when you held the glass, the way a real vine moves when wind catches it.

That liveliness—Bram believed this the way some people believe in God—lived in his hand and nowhere else.

He'd had apprentices. Seven of them over thirty years. They learned to sift sand, tend the furnace, gather molten glass, shape the rough form of a goblet before Bram took over for the engraving that made it *his*. Every one of them left his workshop with a solid education in the fundamentals of the trade. Not one of them ever touched the finishing wheel on a piece that would bear Bram's name.

Several opened their own workshops afterward. Competent places. Well-regarded. But none of them—Bram said this often enough that half the quarter had heard him say it—ever produced stemware that matched what came off his own wheel.

He took that as proof.

What if it wasn't?

What if the real reason none of his former apprentices ever matched his work was that he'd never actually *taught* them the part that mattered, because he'd convinced himself it couldn't be taught in the first place?

I'm going to let that question sit for a moment, because Bram spent thirty years not asking it, and I think you need to feel the weight of that gap before we get to what finally forced it open.

The fall happened on a Tuesday morning in early autumn. Bram had refused to hire someone to fix his workshop's roof—he believed, as a general principle, that a man ought to manage what he could manage himself—and the ladder had other ideas.

Four months. That's how long the healer told him his hand would need before it could hold a tool with anything like the steadiness engraving required. The bones would knit, but slowly, and any weight or precision work before then risked setting them wrong.

The season's commissions didn't pause.

Bram had a full order book. Weddings. Merchant contracts. A standing quarterly order from three harbor inns that had been buying his stemware for a decade. And for the first time in thirty years, he couldn't finish a single piece to the standard his name guaranteed.

You might be thinking: why didn't he just hire it out? Find another engraver, subcontract the work, keep the orders flowing?

Because that wasn't the point. The point—the thing Bram had built his entire reputation on, the thing he'd defended in a hundred small arguments over three decades—was that his name on a piece meant *his hand* had finished it. Not someone approximating his style. Not a competent substitute. Him.

Take that away, and what was left?

He came to the Long Kiln in the second week after the injury. I remember it clearly, because I'd rarely seen Bram bitter, and that day he was. He asked me—not quite looking at me when he said it—whether I thought a workshop could survive a season selling nothing at all rather than selling work beneath its own name.

I told him I didn't know. I'd never watched a workshop as singularly built around one man's hands try to answer that question before.

What I *did* tell him was that Ivo Meer had once nearly lost everything trusting borrowed coin to grow faster than his craft could support, and that trusting another pair of hands, at least, carried a different kind of risk. A risk you could test. On a small piece. Off the books. Before you ever asked it to bear the weight of your full reputation.

Bram's eldest apprentice at that time was a woman named Wilna Draeth.

She'd been with him six years. Six years of watching his hand work. Six years of sifting sand and tending the furnace and shaping rough glass and never—not once—being allowed near the finishing wheel when it mattered.

In the second week of his injury, Wilna offered to try.

One goblet. A trial piece. Off the books entirely. Just so Bram could see for himself whether six years of watching had taught her anything transferable, or whether the liveliness he believed lived only in his fingers truly couldn't survive being asked of anyone else's.

He agreed. Not because he trusted her. Because he was desperate.

And he stood over her the entire time.

I imagine he stood the way he'd once been stood over himself, decades earlier, when he was the apprentice and someone else's reputation hung on whether his hand would steady or slip. Watching her hesitate at the stem's first curve. Watching her correct. Watching her hesitate again.

The goblet she produced wasn't equal to his finest work.

Bram said that clearly, later, and I believe him. It wasn't perfect. The line wavered in two places where his never would have. The spiral's tightness varied slightly from top to bottom in a way that suggested uncertainty rather than deliberate rhythm.

But it was—and this is the part that clearly surprised him—*genuinely good.*

Recognizably built from the pattern he'd spent thirty years refining. Carrying a real, if slightly less confident, version of the same liveliness he'd always assumed was his alone to produce.

Not his hand.

But his pattern, alive in someone else's fingers.

Here's what I think was happening in Bram's head for those thirty years, and here's why I think it matters to anyone reading this who's ever built something they're afraid to let anyone else touch.

Bram had conflated two entirely different things: the skill in his hand, and the *pattern* that skill had refined over three decades of correction and adjustment. He thought they were the same thing. He thought the liveliness in the vine lived in his muscles, his particular way of holding the tool, some ineffable quality that couldn't be extracted or transferred.

What he'd never tested—what he'd actively avoided testing for thirty years—was whether that liveliness might actually live in the *standard* itself. In thirty years of knowing exactly what made a line feel alive versus dead. In being able to *see* the difference and name it and correct it.

And whether that kind of knowing—if you taught it explicitly, deliberately, instead of just demonstrating it while your apprentice watched from three feet away—might be transferable after all.

He'd built a ceiling over his own workshop and called it integrity.

And the only reason he finally discovered it was a ceiling, not a law of nature, was because a wet roof and a slipped ladder forced the question he'd spent three decades not asking.

"I had convinced myself," Bram told me later, after his hand had healed enough to work again, "that the vine lived in my fingers and nowhere else. Because I had never once tested whether it might live, instead, in thirty years of watching and correcting, passed down properly to someone patient enough to receive it."

He paused. We were standing outside the Long Kiln. I remember the light was going gold the way it does in late autumn, and Bram looked older than I'd seen him look before.

"I had simply never taught anyone properly enough," he said, "or trusted anyone long enough, to find out which was actually true."

That sentence has stayed with me.

Because here's the cost Bram paid for thirty years of not testing that question: he capped his entire working output at whatever his own two hands could produce. Every piece he *could* have made, every apprentice who *could* have carried his standard forward while he was still alive to teach it, every expansion his reputation *could* have supported—gone. Not because the craft couldn't scale. Because he'd convinced himself it couldn't, and never ran the experiment that would have proved him wrong.

And he'd called that caution. Integrity. A principled stand against compromising quality.

When really, it was just fear he'd never named.

Bram didn't go back to his old method once his hand healed.

He trained Wilna. Formally. Deliberately. Walking her through every specific correction and adjustment he'd spent thirty years making instinctively without ever once naming them aloud. Within two years, he'd trained a second senior apprentice the same way.

It was slower than doing the work himself. There were weeks—Bram admitted this to me—when he was certain he was wasting time better spent at his own wheel.

But three years later, his workshop was producing nearly triple the finished stemware it had ever managed under his own hands alone. Three sets of trained hands instead of one. And the quality—by Bram's own account—was close enough to his original standard that buyers along the harbor road increasingly couldn't tell which pieces had come from which pair of hands.

I asked him once, years later, whether it bothered him. That his name no longer guaranteed his own personal touch on every piece.

He thought about it longer than I expected.

"It bothered me the whole of that first year," he said finally. "I've come to think I mistook my own hand for the thing my reputation was actually built on. When it was always the pattern. The standard. Thirty years of correction that the pattern demanded. And a pattern properly taught can live in more than one pair of hands at once."

He looked at me. "The same way the Long Kiln's rules have outlived every keeper who's ever tended it. Yours and your father's both."

Then he said something I've thought about often since.

"I don't think I lost anything true when I finally let Wilna near the wheel. I think I only lost the fear that had kept me from testing, thirty years too late, what I had actually built."

Ivo Meer, hearing Bram's story some years later, told me he thought the two of them had learned the same lesson from opposite directions.

"I borrowed capital I didn't yet have the trade to support," Ivo said, "and nearly lost everything to a lender's patience running out before my business caught up. Bram refused to borrow trust he didn't yet know whether his apprentices could support, and nearly capped his whole working life rather than risk finding out."

He paused.

"I think we both needed to learn that growing past what a single pair of hands can hold requires trusting something outside yourself. Coin from a patient lender. Or skill from a patient student. And the trick—in either direction—is testing that trust on something small enough to survive being wrong about it, before you ever ask it to carry the whole of your name."

So here's what I want you to sit with.

Not the lesson about delegation. Not the moral about humility or letting go or trusting your team.

The question Bram didn't ask for thirty years:

What if the thing you're protecting—the thing you've convinced yourself can only live in your own hands, your own judgment, your own irreplaceable presence—isn't actually as fragile as you think it is?

What if it's the *standard* that matters, not the hand? The pattern, not the individual execution? The correction you've learned to see instantly, not the specific fingers doing the correcting?

And what if the only thing standing between you and finding out is that you've never once tested whether the thing you built could survive being taught to someone else who cares enough to learn it properly?

Bram discovered the answer by accident, because a ladder slipped and broke his hand and forced the question before he was ready for it.

You don't have to wait for the ladder.

You could test it now. On something small. Off the books. Just to see whether what you've been calling a principle is actually a principle, or just a ceiling you've been mistaking for the sky.

But here's the part Bram would want me to tell you, and the part I think matters most:

He didn't discover, in his fifty-third year, that Wilna had secretly been capable all along.

He discovered that he'd never given the pattern a real chance to live anywhere but his own two hands.

And the thirty years he spent calling that fear a principle? Those years didn't come back.

XVIII. The Unmarked Blue

The bowl looked right. That was the problem—it mirrored Isbet Voll's signature style so perfectly that it raised more questions than answers.

The bowl held a shade of blue that hummed with familiarity, but it lacked the depth and complexity of Isbet Voll's work—it wasn't a secret she'd unlocked, but one she'd imitated.

The trader who brought it back to Ashmere — a man named Pell, weathered and sharp-eyed, who'd been hauling Isbet Voll's work inland for the better part of a decade — set it on her workbench without ceremony and waited. Didn't say a word. Just stood there with his arms crossed while she reached for it.

I was sorting annealing schedules on the far side of the workshop, close enough to watch but trying not to look like I was watching. Isbet picked up the bowl. Turned it slowly in the late afternoon light streaming through the high windows. Held it close to her face, tilting it so the blue caught the sun. I saw the exact second her expression changed. Saw her fingers tighten on the rim.

"Where?" she said. Just that one word.

"Market town, five days northwest," Pell said. "Man selling it under your name. Had three more just like it on his table. Would've bought them all to get them off the road, but I figured you'd want to see one first."

Isbet set the bowl down. Her hand didn't leave it. One finger traced the rim the way you touch something that shouldn't exist but does. "It's not mine."

"I know that," Pell said. "Question is whether anyone buying it five days from here knows it."

They didn't. That was obvious even before Isbet said it out loud. And why would they? If you've never been to Ashmere, never seen Isbet's actual workshop, never held a genuine piece of her blue glass in your own hands — if all you have to go on is a trader's word and a color that looks close enough in the dim light of your own kitchen — how exactly are you supposed to tell the difference?

You can't. And that's what Isbet stared at for a long time that afternoon, turning that counterfeit bowl over and over in her hands: not the bowl itself, but the shape of the problem it represented. The gap between what she'd built and what someone else could borrow just by saying her name out loud.

Here's what I didn't understand at first, watching her work through it. I thought she was angry. Wouldn't you be? Thirty years of careful, unglamorous work — mixing batches, refining the mineral balance one failed attempt at a time, building a reputation for quality through sheer stubborn consistency — only to have some stranger a week's travel away pocket the profit from your name without ever doing the work that earned it?

But Isbet wasn't angry. Or if she was, anger wasn't the thing driving her thinking. She was troubled. The way someone gets troubled when they realize a problem is bigger and stranger and more tangled than they'd assumed it could ever get, and they're going to have to think their way through it instead of just hitting it harder.

"I built this name so it could travel," she said to me that evening, after Pell had left and the workshop had gone quiet. "That was the whole point. My hands can only make so many pieces in a year. A hundred bowls, maybe. Two hundred if I push it and sacrifice sleep.

But my name, if it's any good, can travel to households I'll never visit. Carried by traders I'll never meet. That's what a reputation is supposed to do."

She stopped. Set the bowl down. Picked it up again.

"But the same thing that lets it travel that far is the thing that lets someone else borrow it. And I never thought about what happens when those two things are the same thing."

The man selling the counterfeit blue was named Colm Ash. Isbet learned that later, though she never met him. He operated well inland, far enough from the coast that no one in his market had ever seen the Cinderquay. They'd never walked past Isbet's workshop or watched smoke rise from her furnace or talked to anyone who'd actually commissioned a piece from her. They just knew the name. Heard it from a trader, maybe. Or from a neighbor who'd heard it from someone else. Description stacked on description until the actual thing became harder to picture than the idea of it.

Colm Ash had figured out — and I want you to notice how brutally simple this was, because the simplicity is the point — that he could buy passable imitations of Isbet's blue from a cheaper glassblower near his own home, mark them up as genuine Cinderquay work, and pocket the difference. The margin on each piece was smaller than what Isbet herself charged, which made it feel like a bargain to the buyer. And the margin on overhead was enormous, because he'd never spent fifteen years learning how to coax that particular blue from the right combination of minerals and heat.

Was it a perfect match? No. Any trained eye could spot the difference. The color was close but not quite right — a little flat, missing that depth Isbet's blue had when you held it up to the light. The weight was wrong. The finish was duller.

But Colm Ash wasn't selling to trained eyes. He was selling to ordinary households who'd heard of Isbet Voll's blue the way you hear about anything famous that comes from far away — secondhand, thirdhand, passed along until it's more legend than fact. In that kind of market, "close enough" is close enough.

And here's the part that kept Isbet up at night. The thing that worried her more than the lost sales, more than the insult of it.

What happens to your reputation when someone buys what they think is your work, and it disappoints them?

Let me walk you through it. You're a household five days from Ashmere. You've heard about this blue glass everyone talks about. Beautiful color, holds up season after season, worth the extra coin. A trader comes through. Says he has some. You buy a piece. You take it home. You use it.

And then, six months later, you notice it's dulling. Streaking. The blue that looked so rich when you first held it is starting to look washed out. It's doing exactly what cheap, poorly annealed glass does when it wasn't made right in the first place — when someone rushed it through the fire, skipped the slow cooling, cut every corner they could to keep the cost down and the volume up.

What do you conclude?

You don't think, "I must have been sold a counterfeit." Why would you? You've never seen a genuine piece to compare it to. You have no idea what Isbet's actual work feels like in your hands, how it catches the light, what it weighs. You think, "Well. I guess the famous Isbet Voll blue isn't as good as everyone said."

And the next time someone mentions her name, you say so. You warn your neighbors. You carry that disappointment back into your household's entire understanding of a name you never actually had the chance to judge fairly. You become, without meaning to, an evangelist for a conclusion that's completely wrong but feels completely true because it's based on your own direct experience.

That's what Isbet was staring at. Not theft — though it was theft. Not lost income — though that was real too. She was staring at the slow, quiet erosion of something she'd spent three decades building, happening in markets she couldn't see, among buyers she'd never meet. And she'd had no idea it was happening at all until Pell walked in with that bowl.

You might be thinking: Couldn't she just go after Colm Ash? Sue him, report him, make him stop?

She considered it. Spent weeks asking around — discreetly, because she didn't want to draw more attention to the problem — about what kind of legal reach a Cinderquay glassblower had over a trader operating five days inland. The answer, as it turned out, was not much. The kind of pursuit that might actually work would cost her more in time and money and workshop attention than she could ever recover. And even if she won — even if she somehow got Colm Ash to stop, paid for the travel and the lawyers and the whole grinding process of proving in some distant magistrate's hall that those bowls weren't what he'd claimed they were — it wouldn't help the households who'd already bought the fakes.

They'd still be walking around thinking Isbet Voll's blue was overrated. They'd still be telling their neighbors the same thing. And Colm Ash's counterfeit operation, even if she shut it down, had already planted that idea in a market she might never reach again.

"Chasing him fixes nothing for the people he wronged," Isbet said. "And there'll be another Colm Ash eventually. There always is, once a name gets valuable enough. I can't chase every one of them individually across every market my reputation has managed to reach. I'd spend the rest of my life doing nothing but that."

So what do you do instead?

Isbet turned that question over for most of a season before she landed on an answer. I watched her work through it in real time — saw her try and discard half a dozen approaches that didn't quite hold. She considered lowering her prices, which would've made counterfeiting less profitable but also would've cheapened the work itself. She considered stopping sales to distant markets entirely, which would've solved the counterfeit problem by killing the reputation altogether. She considered trying to formalize some kind of trader certification system, which collapsed the moment she realized she had no way to enforce it at distance.

And when she finally told me what she'd decided, I'll admit I thought it sounded almost too small to matter.

She was going to add a mark. One tiny initial, no bigger than a grain of sand, worked into the base of every genuine piece at the moment of final shaping. Somewhere an imitator working from borrowed reputation rather than actual skill wouldn't think to look. Somewhere a buyer could check for themselves, if they knew to look for it.

That's it. That's what she came up with after weeks of deliberation. A mark you could barely see unless you turned the piece over and held it up to the light.

I didn't say it out loud, but I remember thinking: A mark? That's the solution? What's to stop someone from just copying the mark too, once they figure out it exists?

Isbet must have seen it on my face, because she answered the question I hadn't asked.

"Nothing stops them forever," she said. "Once enough people know what the mark proves, someone will figure out how to fake it. I'm not trying to build something unbreakable. I'm trying to make the forgery require actual effort. Real skill. Because a fake that costs nothing to produce and nothing to pass off will always spread faster than a fake that forces you to learn something true about my work first."

She paused. Ran her thumb across the base of the counterfeit bowl, where a mark should have been and wasn't.

"Right now, Colm Ash can sell my name without knowing anything about my process. He doesn't need to understand mineral balance or annealing schedules or how long you have to hold the gather at temperature to get the color to set right. He just needs something that looks approximately blue and a willingness to lie about where it came from. That's cheap. I can't compete with cheap by being cheaper. But I can make the lie more expensive. Make it cost him something to maintain."

She didn't announce the mark all at once. Didn't make a big show of it, didn't send out proclamations. Just started mentioning it, quietly, to every household that bought from her directly and every trader she trusted. "Genuine work carries this mark, worked in at shaping, not added after. If it's not there, it's not mine, whatever anyone tells you."

Word spread the way useful information spreads when it actually helps people avoid getting cheated. Slowly at first. A buyer here, a trader there. Then faster as more people learned to check. And within a year, something shifted.

Colm Ash, confronted by a household that had learned to look for the mark and found his stock lacking it, lost enough local reputation that he stopped dealing in counterfeit blue altogether. Whether from shame or simple lost profit, Isbet never found out. Didn't much care to. The point wasn't punishing him. The point was making the deception expensive enough that it stopped being worth his time.

But here's what struck me, watching this whole thing unfold. Most craftsmen in the Cinderquay, wronged the way Isbet was wronged, would have spent their energy on anger. On tracking down the person who stole from them and making them pay. Making an example. Making sure everyone knew what had been done to them and who did it.

Isbet spent hers on building a verifiable proof that didn't require anyone to trust her word over a stranger's.

"I could've just told people to trust me," she said once. "Wouldn't have helped at all. A buyer five days from here has no way of judging whose word to trust between two strangers they've never met. I'm claiming the blue is mine. Colm Ash is claiming it too. Why should they believe me over him? I'm asking them to take it on faith. That's not a position of strength. That's begging."

She held up the bowl, tilted it so I could see where the mark would go.

"What I could give them was something they didn't need to take anyone's word for. Something they could check themselves. A proof, not a promise."

That's a different kind of trust. Sturdier one, too.

I'll tell you what I think this story is actually about, because I don't think it's just about glass.

Every business that grows past what one person can directly control runs into this problem eventually. Your reputation starts traveling to places you've never been. People start buying based on what they've heard, not what they've seen. And the minute that happens — the minute your name is worth something to people who've never met you — it becomes worth something to people who want to borrow it without earning it.

You can spend your energy chasing every fraud individually. Trying to control every mention of your name in every market you've ever reached. That's one approach. I've watched businesses exhaust themselves trying. Pour years into legal battles, tracking down every counterfeit, sending cease-and-desist letters to operations they'll never actually shut down because the jurisdiction is wrong or the cost is too high or the whole thing just moves to a different market the moment you get close.

Or you can do what Isbet did. Build something verifiable into the work itself. Something a buyer can check without needing to know you personally or trust a stranger's word about where something came from.

The interesting question — and I'm going to leave this one hanging for a minute, because I think it's worth sitting with — is what that actually looks like in your business.

Not Isbet's mark. Yours.

What's the equivalent of that tiny initial worked into the base at shaping, so small you'd miss it if you didn't know to look, but unmistakable once you do? What's the thing you can build into your work that proves it came from you without requiring anyone to trust your word that it did?

Because here's what I know from watching Isbet navigate this, and from watching too many businesses since then try to solve the same problem without understanding what they're actually solving. The businesses that survive contact with their own success aren't the ones that never get counterfeited. They're the ones that make the counterfeit expensive enough to catch.

Other glassblowers in the Cinderquay noticed what Isbet had done. Watched it work. Within a decade, half the established masters in the quarter had adopted some version of the practice. Each chose their own distinct mark, plain enough for a distant buyer to learn at a glance. Marl Ashen took it up after a trader tried the same trick with cheap imitation floats stamped with nothing to distinguish them from his own work. Others followed. Not because anyone told them to. Not because they formalized it or held a meeting or issued guidelines. Good practical ideas spread through the Cinderquay the same way they spread everywhere else: quietly, workshop to workshop, each person borrowing the sense of it without needing permission.

Tamzin asked me once, years later during her own training, whether the Long Kiln ought to consider something similar. Some way of marking work that came through our annealing process, in case a dishonest keeper elsewhere tried to claim a piece had been properly tempered when it hadn't. I told her I didn't know if the Long Kiln's trust could be forged quite the same way a single glassblower's mineral mixture could, since our fire served the whole quarter openly rather than any one name privately.

But the underlying lesson held regardless.

A name, once it travels far enough to do you any real good, travels exactly as far as it can be borrowed by someone with no right to it. The craftsman who builds nothing to prove the difference is trusting every stranger in every distant market to have come by it honestly.

That's a lot more trust than any reputation, however earned, can actually afford.

I think about that counterfeit bowl sometimes. The one Pell brought back that started all this. I wonder if the household that bought it ever learned they'd been cheated. If anyone ever told them. If they ever held a genuine piece of Isbet's blue next to the fake and saw the difference for themselves. Or if they're still walking around thinking Isbet Voll's blue just wasn't as good as people said, warning their neighbors off, carrying that disappointment into every conversation about quality and cost and whether the famous version of anything is ever actually worth the price.

I wonder how many other households, in how many other markets, came to the same wrong conclusion about work they never actually saw. How many of them are out there right now, their whole understanding of Isbet's name shaped by something she never touched.

And I wonder — this is the part that kept Isbet up, I think, more than the lost sales or the insult of it — how long you can build something careful and true and excellent before the world's impression of it becomes entirely separate from the thing itself. Before what people think your name means drifts so far from what it actually stands for that the two barely touch anymore. Before your reputation becomes a story people tell about you that has nothing to do with the work you're actually doing.

How long before the fake version of your name — the one that lives in distant markets, passed from stranger to stranger, shaped by every counterfeit and every disappointment — becomes more real to more people than the truth ever could?

Isbet didn't lose her reputation to Colm Ash's counterfeit operation. Not directly. But she came close to losing it to something quieter and harder to fight: her own assumption that work earned honestly would simply be recognized as such, everywhere it traveled, without her ever having to prove it.

The mark didn't solve that problem forever. Nothing does. But it bought her time. Raised the cost of deception just high enough that casual fraud stopped being casual. Made the lie require effort.

So here's what you do on Monday. Before you spend another hour building your reputation wider, ask yourself: What proof am I building in? Not what am I claiming. Not what am I promising people will get if they trust me. What can someone verify for themselves, without needing to take my word for it, that this came from me and not from someone borrowing my name?

Write it down. Make it specific. Make it something a stranger five days away could check.

Because the gap between what you've built and what someone can borrow just by saying your name out loud? That gap doesn't close itself. And the further your reputation travels past the reach of your own hands, the more that gap is going to cost you — unless you've built something into the work itself that makes the difference obvious.

And once you've got that proof worked in, the next question — the one I'm going to leave you holding, because it's the one Isbet's still working through — is this: What do you do when someone figures out how to fake even that?

XIX. The Keeper's Ledger of Cracks

I remember the day Corra Fenn came to the Long Kiln with her dead husband's vase wrapped in cloth, and she asked me a question no glassblower wants to hear.

Corra Fenn's vase was more than just glass; it was a delicate arrangement of memories—each flaw, each imperfection, a weight supporting the whole structure.

And she asked me—her voice so quiet I had to lean forward to hear it over the kiln's low roar—whether I could pull it early. Three days early. So she could have it home in time for what would have been their anniversary.

I said yes.

I have never told anyone this until now. Not my own granddaughter Tamzin, who tends this fire now and who would have every right to ask me why I taught her a rule I didn't always follow myself. Not Corliss Fen, who turned down a wedding feast to honor the same discipline I broke that morning. Not even my own father, who gave me the rule in the first place and never lived to know I'd make this particular exception to it.

The vase held. I checked on it myself years later, at Corra's request, and found it sound—no hairline fractures, no clouding, no sign of the strain I'd risked by rushing its cooling.

But I didn't know it would hold when I made the exception.

I only knew that I could not bear, that particular week, to add a fire's discipline to a woman's grief, and I chose—consciously, deliberately—to break the one rule this entire book has been insisting matters more than any other.

Does that make me a hypocrite?

You might be thinking exactly that. You might be wondering whether anything else I've told you in these nineteen stories can be trusted if the teller himself admits to breaking his own central rule, not out of ignorance or accident, but out of a deliberate choice to value something else more highly in that moment.

I don't know. I've turned the question over for thirty years and I still don't have a clean answer.

What I do know is this: if I'm asking you to build something that lasts, I owe you at least one story where I fell short of my own standard, so you understand that the discipline I'm describing isn't some theoretical virtue I mastered perfectly and now dispense from a position of untouchable expertise. It's a practice I failed at, more than once, and learned from failing.

Let me leave that question hanging for now. We'll come back to it.

Here's what most people don't understand about exceptions: they don't announce themselves as exceptions when they're happening.

They show up dressed as urgent necessities. As special circumstances. As one-time situations where the normal rules don't quite apply because this particular case is different from all the others in some crucial way that makes the usual discipline seem rigid, inflexible, blind to the human reality in front of you.

I kept, across my forty years at the Long Kiln, an informal private accounting—never written down, held only in memory the way Wren Calder once held her sand knowledge on a slate before anyone thought to ask her to keep one—of every piece that came through my fire and cracked, either in the kiln itself or in the weeks and months after, and every piece that came through whole and stayed that way for years afterward.

I didn't keep it out of any scholarly ambition. I kept it because a man who tends the same fire for four decades cannot help but start noticing patterns in what survives and what doesn't, whether or not he ever meant to become a student of the question.

And what I noticed, more than anything else, was this: the pieces that cracked were almost never the ones that looked, on the day they were pulled from the furnace, like the weakest work.

Some of the finest, most skillfully shaped pieces I ever saw pass through my kiln failed within weeks.

A merchant's goblet set, each piece so perfectly matched in weight and clarity that I remember thinking, the morning they came in, that they were the best work I'd seen that season—cracked three weeks later, every single one of them, because the glassblower who made them had been working on borrowed time with a creditor already threatening foreclosure, and the strain of trying to blow perfect work while his entire livelihood was coming apart around him had gone into the glass itself in ways no amount of visible skill could undo afterward.

A decorative window panel commissioned for a guild hall, so intricately worked that two other keepers had turned it down as too fragile to anneal safely—shattered in my kiln on the second night, not because I'd misjudged the timing but because somewhere earlier in its making, someone had rushed the gather to meet a deadline, and the stress had been locked into the piece long before it ever reached me.

And on the other side: some of the plainest, least remarkable pieces I ever weighed through my doorway held for decades. Passed down through households. Outlasted the hands that made them.

A simple water jug, the kind of everyday piece most glassblowers make without thinking about it, that I pulled for a man named Carrick Blythe in my seventh year at the Long Kiln and saw again, still whole and still in use, when his granddaughter brought me a different piece to anneal twenty-six years later.

Why?

Not because it was more skillfully made. Because nothing about its making had ever asked the glass to be something it wasn't ready to be yet.

That's the first thing worth writing down, if you're keeping your own ledger: skill doesn't protect you from strain. Sometimes it hides it. Makes it harder to see until the piece is already cooling and there's nothing left to do but wait and find out whether it holds.

The second thing worth writing down is harder to explain, but I think it matters more.

Every glassblower I've ever known—every single one, myself included—has at least one piece they remember not for how it turned out, but for what they sacrificed to make it in the first place.

Tamsin Greer made hers in her third year of working independently, before she'd built any real client base or reputation. A private commission from a wealthy family, the kind of work that could have opened doors for her if it went well. She was already stretched thin that season, trying to juggle too many smaller commissions to keep her rent paid while also giving this one high-stakes piece the attention it needed.

She told me later—years later, when we were both old enough that the telling didn't cost her anything—that she'd taken on a fourth commission that same month, from a merchant who needed a set of serving pieces for a family celebration, because she couldn't afford to turn down the fee.

"I knew I didn't have time for it," she said. "I knew it was going to pull attention away from the guild piece, which was the only one that actually mattered for my future. But the merchant was paying half upfront, and I needed the money that week or I wasn't going to make rent, so I told myself I could manage both."

She couldn't.

The guild piece came out fine—good enough that the family accepted it without complaint—but not exceptional. Not the kind of work that makes someone remember your name and recommend you to their friends. The merchant's serving pieces came out rushed, a little uneven, and she spent the next two years living down a reputation for inconsistency that started with that single overstretched month.

"What kills me," Tamsin said, sitting across from me in her workshop that evening, "is that I knew. I knew the week I said yes to the merchant that it was the wrong call. I could feel it in my gut. But I couldn't see any other way through the month, so I told myself it would be fine, and by the time I admitted it wasn't fine, I'd already locked myself into a situation where both pieces were going to suffer."

Do you know that feeling?

The one where you can see, clearly, that the thing you're about to say yes to is going to compromise the thing that actually matters, but you say yes anyway because you can't see any other way through the immediate pressure in front of you?

That's not a failure of discipline. That's a failure of knowing, in the moment, which pressure is the one that will actually crack you if you let it build.

I think most fortunes don't fail from lack of opportunity. They fail because the person building them couldn't tell the difference between a necessary long-term investment and an expensive distraction, and by the time they learned the difference, they'd already run out of runway.

Tamsin's mistake wasn't taking on too much work. Plenty of glassblowers survive overstretched seasons. Her mistake was taking on the wrong work—the kind that looked like it was solving her immediate problem but was actually making her long-term problem worse.

The merchant's commission gave her the rent money she needed that week. But it cost her the attention she needed to make the guild piece exceptional, which cost her the reputation she needed to stop scrambling for rent money every month, which meant she spent the next two years still taking commissions she didn't have time for because she still couldn't afford to turn down the immediate fee.

You see the shape of it?

One decision that looked, in the moment, like the only rational choice available—because it was solving a real, immediate problem that genuinely needed solving—turned into a pattern that kept recreating the same problem, over and over, because the solution itself was preventing the deeper foundation from ever getting built.

I watched Tamsin repeat that pattern for almost three years before she finally broke it. And breaking it didn't look like some dramatic moment of clarity or resolution. It looked like her turning down a commission from a merchant who was offering double her normal fee for a rush job, on a week when she genuinely wasn't sure how she was going to pay her supplier.

She told me later that she'd stood in her own doorway for twenty minutes after the merchant left, physically sick with the fear that she'd just made a catastrophic mistake, before she finally turned around and went back to working on the long-term piece she'd been putting off for weeks—a speculative set of goblets in a new style she'd been wanting to try, that had no guaranteed buyer and no immediate payoff, but that she knew, somewhere deeper than rational calculation, was the kind of work that could actually change her trajectory if she gave it the time it needed.

The goblets took her five weeks. She sold them eight months later to a guild master who'd seen them displayed in her workshop window, and the commission that came from that single sale kept her workshop running for the next year and a half.

But she didn't know that would happen when she turned the merchant down.

She only knew that she was tired of solving the same crisis every month, and that the only way to stop solving it was to stop making the choices that kept recreating it, even when those choices looked, in the moment, like the only rational option available.

Here's the question I want you to sit with before we go any further: what is the crisis you keep solving, month after month, that's preventing the foundation from ever getting built?

Not: what's hard right now. Not: what feels urgent. What is the pattern—the specific, recurring shape—of the problem you keep having to solve, over and over, because the way you solved it last time didn't actually make it go away, just pushed it forward another few weeks?

For Tamsin, it was rent. For Ossett Bray, in an earlier chapter, it was the fear that he was falling behind his rival. For Isbet Voll, it was the clients who kept asking for her blue before she'd learned to make it reliably.

The crisis itself doesn't matter as much as the pattern. What matters is whether you can see the difference between a problem that needs solving and a symptom of a deeper structural issue that's going to keep producing the same problem until you stop treating the symptom and start building the foundation.

Most people can't see the difference in the moment.

I couldn't, for most of my working life. I'd look at a client standing in my doorway asking for an early pull and I'd see a single decision: say yes or say no. I didn't see the pattern underneath it—the question of what kind of keeper I was becoming, one choice at a time, depending on which pressures I let override my own judgment and which ones I held the line against.

That's what I mean by a ledger of cracks.

Not a record of failures. A record of which kinds of pressure you let fracture your foundation, again and again, until the fractures compound into a structural weakness you can't see from the outside but that's going to bring the whole thing down the first time it gets tested under real weight.

I think, before I go further, of my own father's last working winter, since I've quoted his single piece of advice throughout this book without ever quite telling you the man himself.

He kept the Long Kiln for thirty-one years, two fewer than I eventually managed, and spent his final season training me the way I later trained Tamzin—patiently, repetitively, correcting the same small errors of attention week after week without ever once raising his voice about it.

He was not, by nature, a warm man. Or at least not one who showed warmth in any way I recognized as a boy. He didn't praise me when I got something right. He didn't put a hand on my shoulder or tell me he was proud of me or do any of the things I told myself, in my more resentful moments, that other men's fathers did for them.

What he did do was say the same handful of things to me, calmly, dozens of times over, rather than simply telling me once and letting my own mistakes teach me the rest.

"The fire does not care how badly a person needs a thing sooner."

He said it in exactly those words, maybe forty times across my first two years working beside him. I counted once, out of sheer irritation, because I thought if I could prove to him how many times he'd already said it he might finally stop repeating himself and trust that I'd learned it.

I was nineteen. I thought the repetition meant he doubted my intelligence.

It was only much later—years later, tending the fire myself through my own hard seasons—that I understood what he'd actually been doing. He wasn't repeating himself because he thought I was slow. He was repeating himself because he knew the lesson wasn't the kind of thing a person learns once and then has forever. It was the kind of thing you have to hear forty times, and then live through another forty situations where it applies, before it finally becomes something deeper than a rule you know intellectually but haven't yet internalized into your body's own sense of what's possible.

I didn't think to thank him properly for that patience before he died. I have tried, in the years since, to pay the debt forward to Tamzin instead, on the theory that this is generally the only direction such debts can actually be paid.

But here's what I only understood decades after he stopped repeating it: he wasn't teaching me a rule about cooling times. He was teaching me how to recognize which pressures were testing my foundation and which ones were just noise.

Every time a client came in asking for an early pull, they had a reason. A good reason. A wedding, a festival, a merchant ship leaving port, a family anniversary, a debt coming due, a promise made that they couldn't break without real cost. The pressure was always legitimate. The question was never whether the pressure was real.

The question was whether I was going to let that particular pressure—however real, however sympathetic—override the one thing I knew about how glass actually holds together over time.

My father understood that I was going to face that question forty times a year for the next thirty years, and that I needed to have already answered it, somewhere deeper than rational calculation, long before the moment arrived where someone I liked was standing in my doorway with a genuinely urgent need and a genuinely sympathetic reason for asking me to make an exception.

That's what the repetition was for.

Not to teach me the rule. To make the answer automatic, so I didn't have to re-decide it every time the question came up in a slightly different form.

Except I did make an exception. For Corra Fenn. And I've had to live with the fact that I don't fully know, even now, whether that makes me weaker or just human.

Let me tell you what I think the difference is between a crack and a choice.

A crack is what happens when you let a pressure override your judgment without meaning to—when you say yes because you can't see any other option in the moment, or because the cost of saying no feels unbearable, or because you've convinced yourself that this particular situation is special enough to justify the exception you've been telling yourself you'd never make.

A choice is what happens when you see the pressure clearly, understand exactly what you're sacrificing by giving in to it, and decide—consciously, deliberately, with full knowledge of the cost—that this particular sacrifice is worth making.

I made a choice the morning Corra Fenn came in. I knew I was breaking my own rule. I knew I was risking the piece. I knew I was setting a precedent I'd have to live with afterward—the knowledge that I could hold the line against forty other clients' legitimate needs but not against this one.

And I decided, in that moment, that I could bear the risk of the vase cracking more easily than I could bear adding a fire's discipline to a woman's grief three weeks after burying her husband.

That's different from the compromises Tamsin was making when she kept taking commissions she didn't have time for. She wasn't choosing the merchant's work over the guild piece with full knowledge of what she was sacrificing. She was telling herself, every time, that she could manage both, that this time would be different, that the immediate pressure didn't have to compromise the long-term foundation because she'd just work harder or sleep less or somehow make it all fit.

She was lying to herself about the cost.

I wasn't lying to myself about the cost. I was choosing to pay it.

That's the difference worth understanding, if you're trying to build something that holds.

Tamzin asked me once, in her second year training beside me, how I could bear the not-knowing.

We were standing at the small viewing window of the Long Kiln, late on a winter evening, watching a shape cool inside that might hold for a century or crack within a month, with no way of telling which from the outside. She was nineteen—the same age I'd been when my father was repeating his own lessons to me—and she'd just watched me turn down a client who'd offered to pay double my normal fee if I'd pull his piece a day early.

The client had left angry. Tamzin had been quiet for a long time after.

"How do you stand it?" she finally asked. "Watching that piece cool, night after night, knowing you won't actually know whether it held until weeks from now, maybe months, when it's too late to do anything about it if you got the timing wrong?"

I told her the truth, which is that I never fully learned to bear it in the way she meant. I simply learned, over enough years, to trust the process more than I trusted my own impatience to see the outcome.

"The not-knowing doesn't go away," I told her. "You only stop needing it to go away, because you've watched the fire keep its own counsel often enough to believe it will do so again."

She didn't seem entirely satisfied with this answer at the time. I suspect she'll understand it better at forty than she did that evening, the way I understood my own father's version of it better at forty than I did at nineteen, hearing it first.

But here's what I didn't tell her that night, and what I want to tell you now: the not-knowing is the entire point.

If you could know, in the moment, whether a decision would hold or crack—if you could see into the future far enough to guarantee the outcome before you committed to the patience—you wouldn't need the discipline at all. You could just optimize. You could choose the fastest path to every outcome you wanted and skip all the slow work that didn't produce immediate visible returns.

But you can't know.

That's the condition under which every actual fortune gets built. You can't see far enough ahead to guarantee that the client you turn down today won't be the connection you needed five years from now. You can't see far enough ahead to guarantee that the extra week you're spending on quality nobody asked for will eventually pay for itself in reputation. You can't see far enough ahead to guarantee that the loan you refuse, or the investor you walk away from, or the shortcut you decline, won't cost you the one opportunity that would have changed everything.

All you can do is build in a way that could survive the not-knowing. And then trust that you've built it well enough to hold, even when you can't see the proof yet.

I think this is true of fortunes in exactly the same way it's true of glass.

Corliss Fen's goblets held for eleven years because he let them cool the full two days, even at the cost of a merchant's disappointment. Wren Calder's clarity held for a lifetime because she spent six years learning her sand before she ever touched a blowpipe. Isbet Voll's blue held for twenty-five years because she never let a single spectacular commission replace the slow, unglamorous work of making it reliably, over and over, the same careful way each time.

None of them were spared hard seasons.

All of them simply built, patiently, in ways that could survive one.

Corliss told me once, late in both our lives, that he still remembered the morning he turned down the wedding feast rather than pull his goblets early. We were sitting outside the Long Kiln on a spring afternoon, both of us too old by then to be doing any of the actual lifting, just watching the younger glassblowers carry their work in and out. He seemed genuinely surprised that I'd carried the memory so long.

"I nearly took the early goblets," he admitted. "I want you to know that, since I don't think I ever told you. I stood in your doorway that morning fully prepared to argue you into it, and something in the way you said no—not unkindly, just certain—made me decide the argument wasn't worth having."

He paused. Looked down at his hands, which were gnarled by then, the joints swollen from forty years of holding a blowpipe.

"I've thought, more than once since, about how differently the rest of my life might have gone if you'd said yes instead."

I didn't tell him, that day, that I'd very nearly said yes. That the Long Kiln's schedule that particular week had been unusually light, and I'd genuinely considered, for a moment, whether one exception might do no real harm. I said no in the end because my father had told me, years before, that the fire doesn't care how badly a person needs a thing sooner, and I'd decided, long before that particular morning ever arrived, what I would do the next time someone stood in my doorway asking me to make an exception to a rule that existed for exactly this reason.

But I made a different choice the morning Corra Fenn came in with her husband's vase.

Same rule. Same fire. Different morning, different person, different grief.

So what's the difference?

I've turned that question over for thirty years and I still don't have a clean answer. What I think now—and this is only what I think, not what I know—is that the rule itself was never the point. The point was always the question underneath it: what kind of craftsman do I mean to become, and what am I willing to sacrifice to become that?

Most mornings, the answer was: I'll hold the line. I'll turn down the extra fee, I'll disappoint the client, I'll lose the commission if that's what it costs to do the work the right way.

One morning, the answer was different.

And I've had to live with the fact that I don't fully know, even now, whether that makes me weaker or just human.

But here's what I do know: I made that exception once in forty years. Once. And I've questioned it every year since.

That's the ledger I kept. Not a record of every time I held the line—those mornings blur together after a while, become unremarkable—but a record of the one morning I didn't, so I could keep asking myself whether I'd made a choice or just allowed a crack.

Tamzin asked me, during her final season of training, a question I've turned over more than any other since.

She asked whether I thought a person could actually choose, in the moment, to become the kind of craftsman who holds the line—or whether the choice had, as I seemed to keep insisting throughout these nineteen stories, always already been made earlier, in some quieter hour nobody was watching.

I told her I thought both were true, in a way that didn't fully resolve into a single tidy answer.

A person can decide, in any given hour, what kind of craftsman they mean to become from that hour forward. Kester Doune decided this, late and at some cost, when he finally asked Isbet for her mineral list instead of continuing to guess at it alone. Ossett Bray decided this when he stopped trying to imitate his rival's speed and started building his own slower, sturdier practice instead.

But the deciding itself doesn't finish the work. It only starts a second, slower kind of labor—showing up the same way, hour after hour, season after season, until the deciding has had enough time to become a habit rather than a single resolved evening.

Ossett needed a decade of that slower labor to become, in fact, the careful glassblower he'd decided, on one difficult afternoon, that he wanted to be. The decision mattered. But it didn't spare him the ten years of actually living it out before it became true in his hands and not just in his intentions.

I don't think there's any way to skip that second labor, however sincerely the first decision is made.

Here's the framework I want you to take from this chapter, the thing worth writing down and keeping where you can see it when the next urgent pressure shows up dressed as a special circumstance:

Every fortune has a ledger of cracks. Small compromises that looked, in the moment, like necessary exceptions. Shortcuts that seemed fine just this once. Pressures you let override your judgment because you couldn't see any other way through that particular week.

Most of those cracks don't matter individually.

What matters is whether you can tell the difference between a crack and a choice.

A crack happens when you convince yourself the exception doesn't count—when you tell yourself this situation is special enough that the usual rules don't apply, or that you'll make it up next time, or that the immediate pressure is urgent enough to justify the compromise.

A choice happens when you see exactly what you're sacrificing, understand the cost fully, and decide that this particular cost is worth paying for this particular reason, knowing you'll have to live with the question afterward.

Cracks compound. They create patterns. They turn into structural weaknesses you can't see from the outside until something puts real weight on them and the whole thing comes apart.

Choices don't compound the same way. You can make a choice, question it for thirty years, and still know it was yours to make.

The ledger I kept wasn't a count of how many times I held the line. It was a record of being able to tell, afterward, whether I'd made a choice or just allowed a crack—whether I'd broken my own rule consciously, with full knowledge of what I was risking, or whether I'd lied to myself about the cost and called it an exception.

That's the only accounting that matters in the long run.

Not whether you ever make an exception. Whether you know, clearly and honestly, when you're making one, so it stays a choice instead of becoming a pattern.

I am an old man now. Tamzin tends the Long Kiln, and I spend most of my days in a chair near the east window where I can still see the furnace light if I lean forward, but I no longer carry the weight of deciding what comes out of it and when.

The Cinderquay's furnaces still burn every working morning, the way they always have. I trust they'll go on teaching the same lesson to whoever is paying attention, long after every name in this book, mine included, has cooled to nothing more than a story told beside them.

But before I close this ledger, I want you to do something. Not think about something. Do it.

Go find the compromise you're currently calling an exception.

You know which one I mean. The client you keep saying yes to even though their work pulls you away from the foundation you're trying to build. The shortcut you keep taking even though you can feel, somewhere deeper than rational calculation, that it's creating a pattern you're going to regret. The urgent pressure you keep letting override your judgment because you can't see any other way through this particular month.

Now ask yourself: is this a choice, or is it a crack?

If you had to explain to someone you respect—someone whose opinion of you actually matters—why you keep making this particular compromise, could you do it honestly? Could you say, clearly and without hedging, "I understand what this is costing me in the long run, and I've decided that cost is worth paying for this specific reason"?

Or would you find yourself explaining why this situation is special, why the usual rules don't quite apply here, why you'll make it up next time, why the immediate pressure is just too urgent to do anything else?

If it's the second one, you're not making a choice. You're allowing a crack. And every time you allow it, you're making it easier to allow again, until the exception becomes the pattern and the pattern becomes the foundation, and then you're building your entire fortune on a structure you know, somewhere you're not quite looking at directly, isn't going to hold.

Here's what happens next, if you stop allowing that particular crack:

You won't know, for a long time, whether you made the right call. The immediate pressure will still be there. The urgent need won't go away just because you decided not to compromise this time. You might lose the client, miss the opportunity, watch someone else take the shortcut you refused and seem to get away with it.

And you'll have to sit with the not-knowing—the possibility that you just made a catastrophic mistake, that you held the line at exactly the wrong moment, that the piece you're cooling so carefully is going to crack anyway and you'll have sacrificed the immediate gain for nothing.

That's the condition under which every real foundation gets built.

But here's the other thing that happens: you stop recreating the same crisis every month. You stop solving the same problem over and over because the solution keeps preventing the deeper structure from getting built. You start becoming, slowly, the kind of person who can tell the difference between a necessary long-term investment and an expensive distraction, because you've practiced making that distinction enough times that it starts to become automatic instead of agonizing.

And five years from now, maybe ten, you'll look back at this particular decision the way Corliss looked back at the morning he turned down the wedding feast—not as the moment everything changed, but as the morning you finally stopped lying to yourself about which pressures were testing your foundation and which ones were just asking you to prove you were serious.

The piece might still crack. I can't promise you it won't.

But you'll know, at least, that you didn't add the crack yourself.

Closing Reflection

The last piece I watched crack in the Long Kiln belonged to a woman whose name I never learned.

She'd arrived at the Cinderquay in early autumn, paid her kiln fee in full, and waited three hours by the fire while her piece cooled—or should have cooled. I was tallying receipts at my bench when I heard the particular small *tick* that glass makes when it decides it's done holding its shape. By the time I looked up, she was already gone, the door to the furnace room swinging shut behind her, and on the stone ledge beside the kiln sat two halves of what had, moments before, been a wine goblet of genuinely beautiful proportions. The fracture ran clean through the bowl, straight down the stem, as if someone had scored it with intention.

I knew, without asking, exactly what had happened. She'd pulled it early. Not wildly early—maybe fifteen minutes, maybe twenty. The glass had looked finished. It had looked stable. And she'd had somewhere to be, or a buyer waiting, or simply run out of the particular species of patience that a fire like that one demands, and those fifteen minutes had seemed, in the moment, like a reasonable trade for whatever waited on the other side of that door.

What do you suppose those fifteen minutes cost her?

Not the goblet—that's obvious enough. But what else? The buyer who'd been waiting, if there was one, who now had to be told the piece wasn't ready after all. The reputation of reliability she might have been building, one completed commission at a time, that cracked along with the glass. The internal accounting she'd have to do later, alone, asking herself whether she could trust her own judgment the next time a piece *looked* finished but the fire hadn't released it yet.

The small, quiet erosion of the thing every working craftsperson needs most and can least afford to lose: the certainty that when they say a thing is done, it actually is.

I never saw her again at the Cinderquay. I don't know if she gave up glasswork entirely, or simply found another kiln, or decided the crack had been bad luck rather than rushed judgment and went on pulling pieces early for the rest of her working life. But I have thought about her often in the years since I stepped back from the fire, because her story—nameless, partial, ending in a sound I heard but didn't see—seems to me to contain everything this book has been trying to say, and everything I still haven't managed to say clearly enough.

The nineteen stories I set down here came from forty years of watching people make choices at a furnace that could not be argued with. Some of those choices compounded quietly into fortunes. Others cracked, audibly or silently, in ways that looked like bad luck until you traced the fracture back to its origin and found a single rushed decision, a single miscalculation about what could be safely skipped, a single moment when someone decided that the discipline they'd been holding didn't need to be held quite so tightly just this once.

What I didn't say clearly enough in any of those nineteen stories—what I'm not sure I understood myself until I started setting them down—is how *reasonable* the rushed choice always feels in the moment. Nobody pulls a piece early thinking, "I'm about to ruin this." They pull it early thinking, "It's been long enough. It looks stable. I need to move on." The glass doesn't announce that it needed another twenty minutes. The buyer at the door doesn't know the piece isn't ready. The only thing that knows is the fire, and the fire doesn't speak except in cracks, and by the time you hear the crack, the decision is already behind you.

I have come to believe—and I'm still deciding whether this is reassuring or terrifying—that almost no one ever experiences the moment of making a costly mistake as anything other than making a reasonable decision under pressure. Corliss Fen didn't think he was hiding a dangerous debt. He thought he was managing a temporary cash flow problem that would resolve itself before anyone needed to know about it. Davor Quill didn't think he was pricing himself out of the ordinary work that could have sustained him between commissions. He thought he was charging what his skill was worth. Perrin Sable didn't think he was taking on more shapes than one pair of hands could hold. He thought he was seizing an opportunity that wouldn't come twice.

The discipline I'm circling here—the one the Long Kiln taught me, badly and slowly, across more failed pieces than I've recounted in this book—is not the discipline of *avoiding* rushed decisions. That's easy to say and nearly impossible to do, because in the moment, the decision never announces itself as rushed. The discipline is something harder and more humble than that: it's the willingness to build external constraints that will stop you even when your own judgment says it's fine to proceed.

You know what I mean if you've ever set a timer and walked away from a piece you desperately wanted to check. If you've ever written a pricing formula and refused to discount below it, even for a buyer you wanted badly to impress. If you've ever built a fund you couldn't touch except under conditions you defined in advance, back when you weren't under pressure and could still think clearly. These aren't acts of virtue. They're acts of accurate pessimism about your future self's ability to judge clearly when money is tight, or a rival is winning, or a buyer is waiting, or the glass *looks* finished even though the fire hasn't released it yet.

The people in these nineteen stories who chose well didn't, for the most part, possess stronger wills or clearer judgment than the people who chose poorly. What they possessed was a deeper distrust of their own judgment under pressure, and a willingness to build, in advance, the kind of external discipline that would hold even when they themselves wanted to let it go.

Let me tell you what I wish I'd understood thirty years sooner than I did.

The Long Kiln couldn't teach patience directly. What it could teach—what it taught everyone who tended it long enough—was the cost of impatience, demonstrated over and over in cracked stems and clouded bowls and pieces that looked flawless until they didn't. But here's the part I didn't see for years: the fire was a *substitute* for the internal discipline none of us actually possessed. It was an external constraint we couldn't argue with, plead with, or convince ourselves to ignore just this once. The glass didn't care whether we had a good reason for pulling it early. It cracked anyway, or it didn't, according to rules none of us had written and couldn't change.

Most of us, building most kinds of wealth in most places that aren't furnace rooms, don't have a fire. We have our own judgment, which bends under pressure. We have our own intentions, which are genuinely good right up until the moment they aren't. We have our own assessment of when something is ready, which is almost always too early, because we can see the part that's finished and we can't see the part that's still cooling.

So we need to build our own fires. Not metaphorically—I mean literally, concretely, in the form of external rules and constraints and automatic systems that will stop us from doing the reasonable-seeming thing that our future selves, under pressure, are absolutely going to want to do.

What does that actually look like? Here's what it looked like for me, when I finally stopped trusting my own judgment and started building external constraints instead:

I set a rule that I wouldn't approve any piece for sale until it had sat in the kiln for a minimum time based on its weight and thickness—not based on how it looked, not based on whether the buyer was waiting, but based on a formula I'd written down when I wasn't under pressure to deliver anything. I posted that formula where I could see it. And then, on the days when a piece looked obviously finished and the buyer was at the door and the extra thirty minutes felt like pure waste, I didn't ask myself whether the piece needed more time. I looked at the formula. The formula didn't care about the buyer at the door.

I set a pricing floor below which I wouldn't accept any commission, and I wrote it in the front of my ledger in ink I couldn't erase. And then, on the seasons when work was scarce and someone offered me something just below that floor, I didn't ask myself whether this particular circumstance justified an exception. I opened the ledger. The number didn't move.

I built a fund for seasons when the kiln work dried up, and I set a rule about what would constitute a legitimate withdrawal—and then I put the fund somewhere I'd have to take three separate deliberate actions to access it. Not because I didn't trust my reasons for wanting the money. Because I didn't trust my ability to tell the difference between a genuine emergency and an urgent-feeling expense that could wait.

None of this is revolutionary. None of it is new. But I'll tell you what surprised me: how much I *resented* these constraints the first dozen times they stopped me from doing what I wanted to do. The piece that looked finished but the timer said wasn't. The commission that felt important but the pricing floor said no. The expense that felt urgent but the fund rules said didn't qualify. Every single time, I was convinced I was right and the rule was being needlessly rigid.

And then, months or years later, I'd look back and see that the rule had been correct and I had been wrong, and that if I'd trusted my in-the-moment judgment I'd have cracked something I couldn't repair.

The humbling part—the part I don't think I understood until I started writing this book—is that I *never got better at knowing when to wait*. I just got better at not trusting myself to know.

So here is what I would say, if I could go back and whisper one thing to the younger woman who first stood beside the Long Kiln and thought she'd eventually learn to judge when a piece was ready just by looking: You won't. You'll get forty years older and forty years more experienced and you still won't be able to tell, in the moment, the difference between "this is ready" and "I want this to be ready." What you *can* do—the only thing you can do—is build external constraints now, while you still have the clarity to build them, that will stop you later, when you don't.

I chose these particular nineteen stories out of the many the Cinderquay could have given me because they seemed, together, to trace the shape of that recognition arriving in different forms to different hands. But I didn't choose them as cautionary tales, and I don't think this book has done its work if you finish it believing that only weak people rush pieces or hide debts or chase rivals or spread themselves too thin. Corliss Fen was careful. Davor Quill was brilliant. Perrin Sable was neither lazy nor stupid. They simply met a particular kind of pressure at a particular moment when they didn't yet have an external constraint in place to stop them from making the reasonable-seeming choice that would crack something important.

The question this book has been circling, through goblets and sand and a swan that couldn't be repeated and a furnace built on borrowed ground, is not "What separates the people who build lasting wealth from the people who don't?" The question is: "What separates the people who recognize they need external discipline from the people who still believe their own judgment will be enough?"

Because here is what I have watched, over forty years beside a fire that didn't forgive rushed choices: every single person who built something that lasted did it by building constraints that would hold when they themselves wanted to let go. And every single person who cracked something important did it by trusting, just once, that this particular circumstance was an exception to the discipline they'd been holding.

The fire taught me this slowly, through more cracks than I've recounted here. I'm setting it down now because I've watched enough good lessons die with the people who learned them to want, just once, to hand it forward to someone who might not otherwise stand close enough to a kiln to hear it.

I don't know what kind of wealth you're building. I don't know what external constraints you need, or what pressures you're already under, or what reasonable-seeming choice you're about to make that will turn out, five years from now, to have been the moment everything cracked. But I know this: if you're waiting to feel certain about when to hold discipline and when to let it go, you're waiting for a feeling that doesn't come. What comes instead is pressure, and urgency, and a buyer at the door, and a piece that looks finished even though it isn't, and a choice that will feel, in the moment, entirely reasonable.

The only thing I know to do about that is to build the constraint now, while you can still see clearly, that will stop you then, when you can't.

The Cinderquay's chimneys still smoke every morning. I'm not there to watch them anymore. But somewhere in that furnace room, right now, someone is standing beside a piece that looks finished, trying to decide whether to trust the fire or trust their eyes. I don't know which they'll choose. I just know that whichever they choose, they'll have to live with the shape of that choice for longer than they think.

What will you build, today, that will stop you tomorrow?

About Eleanor Voss

I met Eleanor Voss in Charleston on a Tuesday morning that felt like breathing through wet wool. August heat that stuck to everything. She'd chosen a diner where the air conditioning wheezed and the coffee tasted like it had been brewed during the Clinton administration.

"You want to know why I write the way I do?" She didn't wait for me to answer. That's her style—pose the question, let it hang there while she stirs her coffee with a spoon that's seen better decades. "Let me tell you about Old Man Tiber."

I'd come expecting the usual author interview dance. Instead, she told me about a glassblower whose shop sat tucked behind a row of pastel antebellum houses, smelling permanently of sand and something faintly metallic. No website. No Instagram feed of moody product shots. Just a small workshop where he made simple things: vases, paperweights, bowls. Beautiful in their unpretentious way, but gathering dust on shelves.

"I was twenty-seven," she said, "and absolutely convinced I could fix his business." She smiled, but it wasn't a warm smile. "He hadn't asked me to fix anything. But I'd just finished my MBA, so naturally I knew everything."

She'd shown up at his shop with spreadsheets. Marketing plans. A whole presentation about craft fairs and online storefronts and the importance of disrupting your market. Tiber listened patiently, occasionally polishing a glass bird with a rag. When she finally ran out of steam, he didn't argue.

"He just pointed at a half-finished goblet and said, 'Watch.'"

For the next hour, she watched him prepare. The precise weighing of silica sand. The mixing with soda ash and lime—each ingredient measured not with digital scales but with a weathered wooden scoop and decades of muscle memory. Then the heating, that slow dance with the furnace, coaxing raw materials into molten life.

"He didn't force the glass," Eleanor said. "He persuaded it."

It wasn't about speed. It was about anticipating the glass's resistance, understanding exactly when to add more air, when to rotate the pipe, when to let it cool just enough. He worked with a concentration that felt almost sacred. And then, after what seemed like forever, there it was: a delicate goblet, shimmering with trapped light, impossibly fragile yet undeniably strong.

Eleanor paused. Sipped her terrible coffee.

"You know what I remember thinking?" She didn't wait for me to guess. "How utterly irrelevant my marketing plans suddenly seemed."

Old Man Tiber's shop eventually closed. Not because his work lacked beauty or skill. It closed because he refused to take on debt for a "revamp." He wouldn't borrow against the future to chase a trend. The cost of maintaining a facade of success would consume the very thing he cherished: the quiet, unhurried practice of his craft.

Here's what she didn't say right away, but what I understood only later: that shop haunted her. Not as a cautionary tale about resisting change. As a brutal lesson in distinguishing between investment and distraction.

She leaned forward. "Most businesses don't fail from lack of talent or opportunity. They fail because founders can't tell the difference between those two things. And by the time they learn, they're out of runway."

I've watched it happen to people I care about. The brilliant software engineer who quit a stable job to launch a startup, then spent eighteen months burning through savings on a sleek office space and conference booth displays while the actual product remained half-built. By the time he realized he'd spent all his oxygen on keeping up appearances, there was nothing left to fuel the real work. Last I heard, he was back in corporate, but something in his eyes had gone dim.

Or the family bakery in my neighborhood. Fourth generation, known for sourdough that people drove across town to buy. Then they took out loans for a trendy remodel—exposed brick, Edison bulbs, reclaimed wood everywhere. They started serving avocado toast and cold brew. The sourdough? Same recipe, but they'd cut the rising time by half to meet the new volume demands. Within a year, the line was gone. Within two, the shop was gone.

That's the cost Eleanor wants you to feel in your bones. Not understand intellectually. *Feel.*

What's it like to spend a decade building something real, only to watch it collapse because you mistook activity for progress? What's it like to realize you chased applause when you needed focus? To understand, too late, that you spent your best years performing success instead of building something that could last?

She doesn't write to offer tips or hacks. She built this entire collection—these parables about glassblowers and tide merchants, borrowed furnaces and unmarked blue—out of deliberate frustration with the self-help industry itself. Too much telling, not enough showing. Too much emphasis on feeling good now, not enough on building something that endures.

"I don't claim these stories happened in any harbor town you'll find on a map," she told me. Her coffee had gone cold. She didn't care. "I claim only that the choices inside them happen everywhere. A piece pulled too soon. A rival's secret chased instead of a craft refined. A debt dressed up as a fine showroom."

She paused. Let me sit with that.

"Those choices are happening right now to people very much like the rest of us."

Her stories aren't about people who achieve effortless success. They're about people who struggle, who fail, who learn to live with uncertainty. People who understand the real work isn't building a perfect life—it's building one that can withstand pressure without shattering.

But here's where most people get her wrong. They think she's advocating for some kind of monastic simplicity. A rejection of ambition. She's not.

When I brought up Jeff Bezos—the early days, when he told his hedge fund investors he wasn't interested in short-term profits, only in building something that would last decades—she didn't dismiss it. "He wasn't thinking about next quarter," she said. "He was thinking about what the world would need in twenty years."

That focus. That willingness to ignore the bright, shiny distractions and tend one fire with obsessive attention. That's what she's after.

Think about your own life right now. Not your business, if you have one. Your actual life. Every day you're gathering materials—experiences, relationships, skills—and shaping them into something. You have limited fuel. Limited time. Limited energy.

What are you building?

More importantly: what are you building that doesn't require constant validation or external funding to survive? What part of your life could withstand a year of silence, a year of nobody watching, and still be worth doing?

I'll be honest—when she asked me that, I didn't have an answer. I'd spent the previous three years chasing bylines in prestigious magazines, obsessing over Twitter followers, treating my writing career like a branding exercise. When was the last time I'd written something just because it mattered to me, not because it might get noticed?

She saw it on my face. Didn't say anything. Just waited.

This is what Eleanor does. She poses questions she doesn't immediately answer, forces you to hold the tension. She's doing it to you right now, through these pages. And the discomfort you might be feeling—that's the point.

Because somewhere in that discomfort is the thing you've been neglecting. Not a task on your to-do list. A core part of yourself. A skill you used to love practicing, before you started measuring it against market demand. A relationship that's grown distant because it didn't fit your five-year plan. A value you've compromised in pursuit of looking successful.

What would it take to rekindle that flame?

She doesn't want a grand gesture or an elaborate plan. She wants one hour. This week. Dedicated solely to the thing that doesn't need to perform, doesn't need to scale, doesn't need to disrupt anything except your own patterns of distraction.

One hour of returning to the core kiln. Of tending the fire that actually matters.

Can you do that?

Or—and this is the question she really wants you to sit with—what are you afraid you'll discover if you do?

Also in the Series

Every book in Parable Wisdom stands on its own — read them in any order. If this one was useful, the library continues:

The Merchant's Ledger

The Shepherd's Fortune

The Weaver's Debt

The Miller's Measure